Telepsychics

Other books by Dr Joseph Murphy Published by Manjul

The Power of Your Subconscious Mind

Life Changing Secrets from the Three Masters of Success: Napoleon Hill, Dale Carnegie and Dr Joseph Murphy

Psychic Perception: The Magic of Extrasensory Power

How to Attract Money

Believe in Yourself

Miracles of Your Mind

Techniques in Prayer Therapy

Putting the Power of Your Subconscious Mind to Work

Maximize Your Potential Through the Power of Your Subconscious Mind:

...to Create Wealth and Success

...to Develop Self-Confidence and Self-Esteem

...for Health and Vitality

...for a More Spiritual Life

...for an Enriched Life

Telepsychics

Tapping Your Hidden Subconscious Powers

DR JOSEPH MURPHY

MANJUL

Manjul Publishing House

First published in India by

MANJUL

Manjul Publishing House

• C-16, Sector 3, Noida, Uttar Pradesh 201301- India
Website: www.manjulindia.com

Registered Office:

•2nd Floor, Usha Preet Complex,
42 Malviya Nagar, Bhopal 462 003 - India

Distribution Centres:

Ahmedabad, Bengaluru, Kochi, Kolkata, Chennai,
Hyderabad, Mumbai, New Delhi, Pune

This edition first published in 2014
Tenth impression 2025

ISBN 978-81-8322-506-9

Printed and bound in India by Repro India Ltd.

CONTENTS

WHAT THIS BOOK CAN DO FOR YOU

Everyone possesses the power of Telepsychics, which means constant communication with the various and marvellous powers of your mind. Wherever I go, whether Europe, Asia, Africa, Australia or the various cities in our own country, people tell me of the amazing untapped powers that they have contacted and that have completely transformed their lives.

This book is extremely practical and down-to-earth. It is intended for all those who wish to experience the riches of the mind to bring them the objects of their desires and needs. You can get immediate results by using the laws of your subconscious mind in the right way. You will find simple, practical techniques and easy-to-do programs in every chapter of this book, enabling you to put into practice the act of leading a full and happy life.

Telepsychics teaches you how to meet and overcome the challenges, difficulties, trials and other problems of daily living. It supplies you with special techniques for putting the extraordinary powers within you into operation at once.

The Unique Features of this Book

You will learn how to visualise future events. In case they appear to be negative in nature, to change them through the application of metaphysical powers. You will learn how to develop your intuitive and other psychic powers, which will set you on the high road to freedom and peace of mind. You will learn the superstitious origins of black and white magic and how to neutralise and reject the so-called voodoo curse as well as all other negative suggestions that may be adversely affecting you.

In this book, you will also learn to use powers of extrasensory and psychic perception. You can communicate with so-called 'dead' people and determine whether or not a loved one has actually spoken to you. Many people converse at length with voices of discarnate entities or disembodied spirits and receive extraordinarily intelligent answers. You will learn how a sensitive or psychic person practices automatic writing (without using a pen or pencil) and reveals future events with amazing accuracy.

In writing the many chapters of this book, I had in mind the salesman, the stenographer, the mailman, the housewife, the businessman, the clerk behind the counter, the student, the professional man virtually all those who wish to fulfil their dreams, aspirations and ambitions in life. Therefore, you will find each chapter pregnant with simple, intensely practical techniques, the what-to-do and how-to-do-it, for calling forth the powers of your psychic mind, knowing that there is an infinite intelligence in your subconscious mind that knows only the true answer.

Some of the Highlights of this Book

These are some of the actual case histories in this book that demonstrate how others have benefited from using their telepsychic powers:

- How a college student who was failing in his studies suddenly realised that the Infinite cannot fail – how, tuning in with the Infinite, he became a brilliant success.

- How, in a dream, a young nurse saw the skyjacking of the plane on which she had planned to travel. She cancelled her trip and the plane was subsequently skyjacked.
- How a sales manager focused his attention on a blank wall and then projected onto the wall a mental picture of the annual sales figures that he desired to achieve. He got marvellous results.
- How a woman overcame her fear of four people, who she said were praying for her downfall. She joined up with the One Power and is now at peace.
- How a woman in Hawaii learned to laugh at so-called black magic and voodoo curses. She discovered the Power within her and said, 'I am now free.'
- How a university student who was praying for a husband saw her future husband in a dream with a book under his arm. She met him two months later and married him.
- How telepsychics enabled a detective to discover large supplies of cocaine and heroin. All this was revealed to him in a dream. The value of the narcotics was $3,000,000.
- How a wife used telepsychics and saved her husband's life. A man fired three shots at him, all of which missed him as a result of his wife's protective prayer.
- How telepsychics saved his life in a dream. In his dream he read the headlines in a newspaper which told him of the loss of 92 passengers. He cancelled his flight and the accident that was foreseen in his dream actually occurred.
- How telepsychics saved the lives of a mother and son who were being slowly asphyxiated by the leakage of a gas jet. Her deceased husband appeared to her and told her to turn off the gas.
- How telepyschics revealed a lost diamond. In a dream, she saw her ring clearly in the maid's room, wrapped in a piece of paper and located in an old shoe belonging to the maid.
- How telepsychics acts as an invisible partner and guide to a businessman who frequently invests up to $1,000,000.00 in bonds. His investments are always very profitable.

- How a simple explanation of telepsychics saved the life of a would-be suicide.
- How a man's knowledge of telepsychics saved his life on a burning airplane.
- How a young businessman practiced telepsychics and made a small fortune in gold stock. A man appeared to him in a dream and gave him the names of gold stocks to purchase. He followed the instructions and became financially successful.
- How telepsychics revealed the whereabouts of a lost deed to a young secretary whose father had died, leaving no records.
- How telepsychics revealed hidden talents to a teacher in a dream, fulfilling her heart's desire for full expression and accumulation of wealth.
- How telepsychics revealed to a girl, whose father had died, the whereabouts of hidden family money. Her father appeared to her in a dream and showed her where a steel box, containing $13,000.00[$] was located.
- How telepsychics enabled a young man to become an airline pilot. There were 2500 applicants for ten openings; 90 percent of them had more experience than this young man. He pictured himself working as a pilot. He succeeded to get the position.
- How telepsychics gave the numbers to play on the roulette wheel to a man in his sleep. The next day, he won $50,000.00.
- How telepsychics revealed to a young girl the whereabouts of an old earthenware jug. Her father dug up the backyard and found the jug, which was full of valuable coins dating back to 1898.

Telepsychics is a simple and practical, logical and scientific method that works to fulfil your deepest desires. I want to say positively, definitely, unquestionably and decisively that by using the instructions in this book, you will reap the fruits of a rich, happy, joyous and successful life. Let wonders happen to you by following the guidance of this book and by applying it in your daily life.

Dr Joseph Murphy

1

HOW TELEPSYCHICS CAN BE YOUR MAGIC POWER FOR PERFECT LIVING

Magic is referred to as the art of producing a desired effect or result through the use of various techniques. Men speak of the magic of music, the magic of spring and the magic of beauty. It is also referred to as the art of causing illusions, such as in entertainment, by the use of sleight of hand, legerdemain and conjuring, whereby one pulls a rabbit out of a hat or causes a human being to disappear.

The Invisible Power Within You

To most people, magic is the production of effects by unknown forces. Magic, however, is a relative term. Obviously, if the processes are known to you, the work is not a work of magic to you. In many remote places in the world today, among primitive people, the airplane, radio, television or recording machines would be considered magical objects. Likewise, these discoveries would have been looked upon as magical 150 or 200 years ago in our own country.

We understand how astronauts manage to go to the moon today and do not, therefore, call it magical. All forces are, in their nature, unknown; all things come forth from spirit. We do not see Spirit but we can feel the spirit of joy, the spirit of the game, the spirit of the musician, the spirit of the speaker and the spirit of goodness, truth and beauty moving through our minds and hearts.

No theologian has ever seen Spirit (God) but we can use this Presence and Power in all phases of our lives. We don't know what electricity is, for instance; we only know about some of the things it does. The force itself is still unknown to us. Actually, all of us practice magic constantly. We desire to lift our finger – lo and behold, the invisible power responds according to the intention of our mind; yet we do not know exactly how we move and lift our finger.

Socrates informs us that just by lifting a finger, you disturb the most distant star. You will perceive that we all are familiar enough with the magic power within us, though it is not called by that name in our everyday world.

Tuning In with the Magic Power

You can tune in to the Infinite Power within you and transform your whole life. Wherever I go, whether to Europe, Asia, Africa, Australia or the various cities in our own country, people tell me of the amazing, untapped Power which they have contacted and which has completely transformed their lives. Many of them have said that their old friends and acquaintances have remarked to them, 'What's happened to you? I hardly know you.'

As you follow the techniques and processes outlined in this book, you will find out that this inner Power can solve your problems, make you prosper, reveal hidden talents to you and lift you up from sickness, failure, lack and limitations of all kinds. This Power can guide you and open up new doors of expression for you. You can receive inspiration, guidance and new creative ideas, bringing you harmony, happiness and peace of mind.

How a college student tuned in for passing examinations

A few months ago, I talked with a college student who was getting rather poor grades. He was quite despondent because his marks were, as he said, bad enough to cause him to flunk out. He had been reading and studying *Secrets of the I Ching,** and in asking it a question, it said, 'Go and see the great man.' He interpreted that to mean that he should see a counsellor or spiritual advisor, though it had deeper meanings, also.

I asked, 'Why do you want poor grades? Infinite intelligence is within your subconscious mind and you can use it.'

'Okay,' he said. 'My parents criticise me and point out that my sister is a much better student than I am and passes all her examinations easily.'

I explained to this young man that he should immediately cease comparing himself with his sister, because all comparisons are odious, pointing out that each person in unique and that everyone is born with different endowments.

'In comparing yourself with others, you are placing the other on a pedestal and denigrating yourself. Furthermore, you are giving too much attention to the activities and successes of your sister and neglecting your own studies while forgetting your own inner capacities and abilities. To continue along this line will cause you to lose initiative and incentive, causing a build-up of inner tension and anxiety.'

'The only competition is in your own mind between the thought of failure and the thought of success. You were born to win, to triumph, to succeed and to overcome all problems. The

---

*Dr Joseph Murphy, *Secrets of I Ching* (Parker Publishing Company, Inc 1970)

Infinite Power can't fail and you are one with It.'

At my suggestion, he followed a simple and very practical technique, which he went over mentally every night prior to retiring, as follows:

'I sincerely wish for my sister and all other students in my classes success and accomplishment in all their studies. Infinite Intelligence guides me in my studies and reveals to me everything I need to know. I know my subconscious mind has a perfect memory and reveals to me the answers on all my examinations. I pass all my examinations in Divine order. I sleep in peace every night and I awake in joy.'

As he continued thinking and acting along the above lines, a few weeks ago he said to me, 'I'm competing with no one. I'm doing fine. I know now that I have what it takes.'

As Ralph Waldo Emerson once said, 'There is guidance for each of us and by lowly listening; we shall hear the right word.'

How she practiced telepsychics

Tele means communication and *psyche* means the Soul or Spirit within you. When you pray, you are contacting your Psyche or Higher Self. It responds according to your belief and recognition of It.

A young nurse recently planned on taking a flight but the night before the departure, she had a vivid experience. In a dream, she saw the plane hijacked while an inner voice spoke to her and said, 'Cancel your trip.' She awakened startled but she followed the inner instruction and cancelled the flight. Incidentally, the plane she had selected was hijacked.

The guiding principle of her subconscious caused her to see the event before it happened in order to protect her. The plan to hijack the plane was already in the universal subconscious mind…As she prayed for guidance, she received the answer in a dream, which came from her deeper mind.

Her prayer before retiring every night is as follows:'Divine

Love goes before me wherever I go, making joyous, happy and glorious my way. The sacred circle of God's eternal love surrounds me and I am always watched over by God. I bear a charmed life.'

The above prayer is true telepsychics or actual communication with the infinite intelligence of her subconscious mind, which knows all, sees all. This responds to the nature of her thought. Action and reaction are cosmic and universal. In prayer, you have a dialogue with your Higher Self, which some call God. Others use the term True Self, Living Spirit Almighty, the Father Within, Infinite Intelligence, the Over soul, Brahma, Allah etc. There are many names for the Power within you but, in any case, it is timeless, space less, ageless and nameless. The Bible calls It 'I AM,' which means Being, Life, Awareness, Self-Originating Spirit, Unconditioned Consciousness.

All you need to remember is that your thought causes the Infinite Power to respond; you are dealing with a reciprocal action-and-reaction: as you sow you reap that is, as you call you receive an answer.

He discovered the power of his mental image

Thoreau said years ago that we become what we image ourselves to be. The mental picture you hold in your mind tends to manifest itself in your experience.

A sales manager who often attends my lectures at the Wilshire Ebell Theatre on Sunday mornings told me how he draws on the power of his imagination, which he finds extraordinarily effective. Here it is:

He relaxes and calms his mind by quietly repeating to himself the 23rd Psalm; then he looks at the white wall in his office. As he focusses his attention on the blank white wall, he throws a picture of the sales figures he wants at the end of the year. He looks at the amount closely, focussing all his attention on the financial figures; then he claims these figures are now sinking down into his subconscious mind. Finally, he hears the president of the company congratulating him on the wonderful growth of the organisation as also his splendid accomplishments. He said that he knew when the figures had reached his subconscious, because the impression was always followed by a sense of great peace.

This is truly telepsychics in action: his mental image was communicated to his psyche, (subconscious mind) which was developed in the darkroom of his mind, coming forth as the joy of the answered prayer.

This sales manager said that for the past four years the financial sales figures for each of the years has always exceeded his mental image. This is true, because your subconscious always magnifies whatever is impressed upon it.

Give the Right Mental Image to Your Subconscious

Every picture you create in your mind, particularly when emotionalised, can come to pass. It works out in action, either internally or externally. If you inhibit it from working out in external action, it is inevitable that it will work out in internal action in some mental, emotional or physical disturbance of your body. Be careful that you do not indulge in mental images that you don't want to carry out in external actions.

I once knew an alcoholic who was imprisoned for manslaughter. He said to me that he was absolutely determined never to imbibe alcohol again when he was discharged from prison. The very day he was released, however, he immediately began to drink heavily. Why? The simple reason is because he was always forming mental pictures of a drink while he was in prison and the moment he got out he took to the bottle. He externalised the act of anything he was picturing all the time. If he had not externalised his mental image, this picture would have hurt him in some other way, probably in the form of physical or emotional upset.

Thus, every picture that you create in your mind has to be worked into action, lest it manifest itself in some mental, physical or emotional disharmony in the body.

How a writer discovered the magic power within himself

A writer-friend of mine told me that he had a misunderstanding with the producer of a play based on his script. They had a rather heated exchange. He had read *Miracle of Mind Dynamics** then, had applied many of the techniques of prayer outlined therein. When he went home he went into his den, relaxed and thought about the Infinite Power within him; then he conducted an imaginary conversation with the producer, as if he were experiencing the future now. He pictured the producer right in front of him, claiming harmony, peace and perfect understanding between them. In his vivid imagination he conversed with the producer, saying that all he wanted was Divine right action. He imagined the producer responding, saying, 'There is perfect agreement between us. Divine right action prevails.'

In this quiet, passive state, he envisioned a happy ending, feeling the imaginary handshake of the producer and the perfect harmonious solution. Several days passed. The writer met the producer in the club to which they belonged. Before he had a chance to greet him, the producer called him over and said, 'I have reread your script and I admit you were right. What is right action for one is right action for all concerned.'

What the writer had claimed to be true subjectively came to pass objectively. Try it. It works! There isn't a single human being in the country that cannot overcome fear, anger and hostility to resolve his conflicts, sharpen his mind, indeed live an amazing life. We go about, it by changing our attitudes like the above-mentioned writer. William James, the great American psychologist, said, 'Human beings can alter their lives by altering their attitudes of mind.'

---

*Dr Joseph Murphy, *Miracle of Mind Dynamics* (Prentice-Hall, Inc., Englewood Cliffs, New Jersey, 1964.)

Inspiration or contact with the Infinite Power, can come to you as easily as the air you breathe. You breathe casually and without effort; likewise, we let the Divine intelligence or Creative Essence of God into our minds or intellect without tension.

Many people have erroneous ideas about inspiration; they believe it is an extraordinary experience given or had by mystics or other highly spiritual people. This is not so. Although it is true that people who lead spiritual lives may be inspired frequently or get spontaneous feelings or ideas, it is equally true that the businessman may also become inspired by turning to the Infinite Power within him. Inspiration or Divine guidance, may be had on any problem. In other words, the information you seek, knowledge required or business difficulties solved may be achieved simply by asking God or the Infinite Power, for the answer.

You may be a novelist and have several books to your credit; yet when you get a pad and a pencil or typewriter, you can't begin, nothing happens, not an idea, plot or story. You may drink six cups of coffee and it does not help. Quiet your mind however, to claim that you are inspired from On High and that God's creative ideas unfold within you in Divine order. You will then receive knowledge, guidance and creative energy. Ideas will flow to you freely, joyously and lovingly.

An engineer gets specific data

An engineer once told me that he wanted specific data for an engineering examination. His professor had given him the information but he realised he had forgotten it. He asked his subconscious mind to furnish him with the answer and then went to work on other parts of the examination and the answer welled up from his deeper mind. It was in his subconscious mind all the time. When he relaxed and let go, the wisdom of his subconscious came freely into his conscious mind and he passed his examination easily. Remember: the quiet mind receives the answer.

The cash register man

Some years ago I read a magazine article about the man who got the idea for the cash register. The article explained that, although the man had not had much of an 'education,' he was very intelligent and perceptive.

Once, while on an ocean voyage, he asked the ship's officer to explain to him the workings of the log, which registered the speed of the ship. The explanation was given – and suddenly, the man got the idea for the cash register!

This man was aware of a specific problem: men are often wrongfully accused of stealing while others steal and never get caught; also, when cash is exchanged, countless errors can be made in change. He immediately related the workings of the ship's log to a solution to this problem and through this inspiration, he developed the cash register.

This was inspiration or telepsychics. Ask you're subconscious to give you creative ideas and a similar idea worth a fortune may well up within you.

How to Practice Telepsychics Every Day

You can tune in with your Higher Self and receive answers by calming yourself and knowing that, when you call, there will be a response in accordance with the nature of your call. Recall that the wire from the power house is placed in your room or cellar. The main wire belongs to Edison, the wiring in the house belongs to you and the contact is there enabling you to turn on the light. Similarly, your conscious mind can, at this moment, contact the infinite storehouse and wisdom within you. You would not pray unless you believed that there is a wisdom and intelligence in your subconscious which knows all and sees all and is responsive to your call.

The Bible says: *Before they call, I will answer; and while they are yet speaking, I will hear.* – Isaiah 65:24

POINTS TO REMEMBER...

1. Telepsychics means communication with your psyche or soul, i.e., your subconscious mind, which is co-extensive with all wisdom and all power. When you pray believing, your subconscious mind responds with the answer.
2. Magic is a relative term. To most people, magic is the production of effects by unknown forces. All forces are, in their essence, unknown. Scientists do not know what energy is. Edison, when asked by a woman what electricity was, replied, 'Madam, it is. Use it.' There is an invisible wisdom, power and intelligence in your subconscious mind which knows all and sees all. You can contact this power with your conscious mind. This primal power is timeless, ageless, nameless and eternal.
3. You can use your inner powers to solve your problems, prosper you along all lines, reveal your hidden talents and set you on the high road to happiness, peace of mind and freedom.
4. Cease comparing yourself with others. This attitude consists in denigrating yourself while placing others on a pedestal. You are unique – different from every person in the world. Give attention to your inner powers and you will excel in your chosen field. If you wish to pass an examination, don't compare yourself with other students; this attitude causes tension and anxiety. Relax, quiet your mind and every morning and night affirm feelingly and knowingly, 'Infinite Intelligence in my subconscious mind guides me in all my studies and I will pass all examinations in Divine order.'
5. When you pray you are actually contacting your Higher Self, which some call God or Supreme Intelligence. You get an

answer according to your belief. Sometimes you may receive an answer in a dream that warns you not to take a certain trip. One young lady who prayed regularly for guidance, Divine love and right action, dreamed 24 hours in advance of the hijacking of the plane on which she had arranged to travel. As a result, she cancelled the trip. The reason for this is simple. The plan of the hijacking was already known in the collective subconscious. Her own subconscious, which is one with the collective mind, revealed the plan to her.

6. The picture you have in your mind tends to manifest itself in your life. A sales manager focuses his attention on a certain financial figure for the end of the year and by repetition and concentration, this mental picture enters his subconscious mind. In the past four years his subconscious has magnified and multiplied the desired result. The subconscious magnifies whatever you give attention to.
7. An ex-alcoholic who pictures himself drinking will be compelled to drink. Any mental picture you emotionalise will come to pass in your experience. Imagine what is lovely and of good value.
8. If you have a misunderstanding with another person, conduct an imaginary conversation with him based on the Golden Rule and the Law of Love, realising that there is harmony, peace and Divine understanding between you. Imagine and picture in your mind the happy ending by shaking hands in harmony and peace. What you imagine and feel to be true subjectively will come to pass objectively. The Bible says:

   I have told you before it come to pass, that, when it is come to pass, ye might believe. – John 14:29

2

HOW TELEPSYCHICS REVEALS THE GREAT SECRET OF THE AGES

Many people today are afraid of malignant thought projections, black magic, the evil eye, voodoo, etc.; there seems to be a general fear that there is some sort of hidden power that others can use to hurt them or to mar their happiness.

The Greatest Secret Within Man

You will truly lead a full and happy life when you awaken to the greatest of all truths. It is expressed in Deuteronomy 6:4: Hear, O Israel: the Lord our God is one Lord, which means Hear (understand), O Israel (illumined, awakened man): the Lord (the Lordly Power or Supreme Power) our God (our Ruler, the Infinite Power) is one Lord (one Power – not two, not three, not ten, not 1000 – just one).

The Superstitious Origin of Black and White Magic

When we were very young and highly impressionable, our parents, who didn't know any better, told us about a punitive God and also about a devil who would tempt us; they also cautioned us that, if we were very bad, we might go to hell and suffer forever. Children and childish minds think only in pictures or mental images and not knowing anything better, they project images of God and a devil. Children envision God up in the heavens on a golden throne surrounded by angels and the devil down below in the flames of hell, not realising that, in fact, all of us create our own heaven and our own hell by the ways in which we think, feel and believe.

Primitive man attributed pleasure to the gods and all pain, suffering and misery to evil spirits or to devils of his own creation. Prehistoric man realised that he was subjected to strange forces over which he seemed to have no control. Earthquakes and floods took place and not knowing the cause, the jungle priests said that the gods were angry; then they proceeded to offer up sacrifices to appease the angry wrath of the supposed gods. The sun gave man heat but in a prolonged drought, the same sun seemed to scorch the earth. Fire warmed man but it also burned him; the thunder terrified him; lightning paralysed him with fear; the waters flooded his lands, at times; his cattle and children were drowned. His understanding of external powers consisted of primitive and fundamental beliefs in many types of gods.

From this crude and ignorant reasoning, primitive man proceeded to supplicate the intelligences of the winds, the stars and the waters, hoping they would hear him and answer his prayer. He proceeded to make offerings and sacrifices to the gods of the wind and the rain.

Primitive man divided the gods and genii into beneficial and malignant powers. Hence, you will find the universality of these two powers in all the creedal beliefs of millions of people. A belief in two powers is a hangover from these age-old superstitious beliefs.

Good and Evil in Your Life Are Determined by Your Thoughts

The forces of nature are not evil; it depends upon how you use them. You can use any power in either of two ways. The same wind will blow a boat on the rocks or carry it safely to the harbour. You can use electricity to fry an egg or to electrocute someone. You can use atomic energy constructively to drive a ship across the ocean or to destroy cities, towns and people. You can use water to drown a child or quench his thirst – fire to warm or burn him. We give purpose to the forces of nature.

Good and evil are in the mind of the individual; they are nowhere else. Think good and good follows; think evil and evil follows.

Keep your eyes on the greatest thought and move ahead in life

Judge Thomas Troward,* author of Edinburgh Lectures and many other books, stated in 1902:

Once you admit that there is any Power outside yourself, however beneficial you may conceive it to be, you have sown the seed which must sooner or later bear the fruit of 'fear,' which is the entire ruin of life, love and liberty. We must contend earnestly, both within ourselves and outwardly, for the one great foundation and never, now on to all eternity, admit for a single instant any thought which is opposed to this, the Basic Truth of Being.

Troward has stated a marvellous truth, which each person should keep before him. The suggestions of others have no power to create the things they suggest. The power is in your own thought. When your thoughts are God's thoughts, God's power

*_Collected Essays of Thomas Troward_ (DeVorss & Company), pp. 166–167.

is with your thoughts of good. It is always the movement of your own thought which is a creative power. You have the power to completely reject any negative suggestion and unite mentally with the Omnipotence within you.

Why the so-called voodoo curse is merely a negative suggestion

Some years ago, I visited Capetown, South Africa, to lecture for the late Dr Hester Brant, who had a large centre there teaching the science of the mind. While I was there, she arranged for me to visit one of the gold mines in Johannesburg.

An English physician affiliated with one of the mines I visited told me that when a man who is working in the mine violates company code, he gets a message from the voodoo doctor such as, 'You will die at 6:00PM,' and he sits down and dies. Post-mortem examinations show no reason for the deaths whatever and the doctor added that fear, generated by the violators themselves, is the actual cause of death.

She was terrified because they were praying against her

A few weeks ago, I talked to a young woman who was in great distress because she said there were some people in her former church praying against her because she had left their group. She believed that she was cursed and that, as a result, everything was going wrong.

I explained to her that the curse she mentioned was really the negative use of the law of her subconscious mind* within herself and that she was imposing the curses on herself through fear. The suggestions of others had become a movement of her own thoughts and since her thoughts were creative, she was hurting herself. She was transferring the power within herself to members

*See *The Power of Your Subconscious Mind,* by Dr Joseph Murphy (Prentice-Hall, Inc., Englewood Cliffs, NJ, 1963.)

of her former church, not realising that they had no power.

I explained to her that the power was within her and that she should immediately cease transmitting the power to others. God or Spirit is One and Indivisible: It moves as unity. There are no divisions or quarrels in It As soon as she aligned herself with the Infinite and gave It her allegiance, devotion and loyalty, nothing would happen to her.

> She began to affirm, '*I dwell in the secret place of the Most High and I abide under the shadow of the Almighty. I will say of the Lord, He is my refuge and my fortress: my God; in Him will I trust.*' (Psalm 91:2)

I added, 'Look at those people as extremely ignorant and have compassion for them. The real and ultimate power is the great affirmative, which is constructive. They are using suggestion, which is a power but not the Power (God) which moves as harmony, beauty, love and peace. Remember, a suggestion has no power unless you give it power. Join up consciously with the Infinite Love, Life and Power within you and constantly realise, 'God's love surrounds me, enfolds me and enwraps me. I bear a charmed life. The spell of God envelops my whole being. Whenever I think of the church people, I will immediately affirm I lose you to God and let you go.'

Practicing the above simple truths, she was at peace and she actually laughed at herself for giving her adversaries power. After about a week or so, she heard that five of these women became extremely ill and that one had passed on. This young woman no longer received their negative thoughts and vibrations and their evil thoughts returned with double force to themselves. This is called 'the boomerang.'

She believed her father used black magic

Some months ago, I listened to the story of a woman in Honolulu who said that she had married outside her race and religion and that, since her father was a Kahuna (native priest) and had magical powers, he was determined through sorcery to break up her marriage.

The explanation is often times the cure. This woman was a graduate of the University of Hawaii and had majored in psychology, yet she lived in fear of her father's curse. I elaborated along these lines, explaining that if love united herself and her husband, no person or condition could break her marriage up. God is love and when two hearts beat as one, all the excommunications and curses of the world would be as papier mâché aimed at a British battleship.

The susceptibility to impressions of our subconscious mind* coupled with the negative use of our imagination has partially paralysed millions of unknowing people. This woman was labouring under the delusion that her father's sorcery (negative use of mind) was potent and would succeed.

I told her the story of Plotinus, who lived over seventeen hundred years ago. An Egyptian priest visited Plotinus, one of the great, illumined men of his age. The priest imposed a curse on Plotinus, that is, he mentally concentrated on a death wish for Plotinus and aimed it mentally at him. Plotinus knew the trick and also knew that the foolish priest thought he had power. There is no power in a negative suggestion or a curse hurled at you by any or all the priests in the world, unless you are foolish and ignorant enough to accept it.

Plotinus sensed his oneness with a God of Love. God is Omnipotent; one with God is a majority.

If God be for us, who can be against us? Romans 8:31

It is recorded that the curse recoiled and finding no place in Plotinus, 'boomeranged' on the Egyptian priest who had tried to

---

*See *The Power of Your Subconscious Mind*, by Dr Joseph Murphy (Prentice-Hall, Inc, Englewood Cliffs, NJ, 1963.)

impose it. He fell into a fit and collapsed at the feet of Plotinus. Plotinus had pity on the priest's ignorance and took him by the hand and raised him up. This priest recognised the One Power and became a devoted disciple of Plotinus.

This explanation took a great load off the mind of this Hawaiian woman. She said to her father, 'Dad, I am no longer afraid of you. You are to be pitied. You think you have power but all you are using are negative suggestions. What you suggest or wish for another, you are creating in your own experience. The power is within m and I know my oneness with God. His love surrounds us and watches over us. Whenever I think of you, I affirm, "God is for me; no one can be against me. I am free."' She blessed her father, loosened his power over her, to let him go.

Shortly afterwards, she wrote me, saying that her father continued to hate her and her husband and had written her that his sorcery or black magic would destroy both of them. She paid no attention to his threats. Within a few weeks, he dropped dead on the street. She said that her father had killed himself with hatred – she was right. Hatred, jealousy and hostility kill love, peace, harmony, joy, vitality and goodwill. All his negative, destructive thoughts recoiled on himself and the double blow proved too much for him. Whatever you wish for another, you create and manifest in your own body and experience.

Moses and the Egyptian Priests

In ancient times, the multitude believed that their priests had the power to curse those who displeased or irritated them and the priests of that day took advantage of the ignorance of the people.

Moses saw through the chicanery and deceit of the Egyptian priests. They were completely dumbfounded by him. Their fear of him caused the priests to abandon their attempts at intimidating Moses and his people.

Moses taught the oneness of the Spiritual Power. The belief and faith of the Egyptians was built on a belief in many powers. Moses knew that God was One and his awareness scattered all negative ideas to the winds.

Become a Straight-Line Thinker

It is absolutely essential that you get this straight: that harmony, beauty, love, peace, joy and all the blessings of life come from the One Source. God cannot do anything unloving, for God is Boundless Love. God cannot wish pain, for God is absolute peace. God cannot wish sorrow, for God is absolute joy. God cannot wish death, for God is Life and that is your life now.

All so-called curses, sorcery, black magic, satanisms, etc., come from the frightfully ignorant belief in a suppositional opposite force. There is only One Power, One God – not two, three or a thousand just one. To believe in an evil power to challenge God is based entirely on a rank superstition.

When men use the One Power constructively, harmoniously, peacefully and joyously, they call it God. When men use the Power ignorantly, negatively and foolishly, they call it Satan, the devil, evil spirits etc.

Curses return home to roost

When you turn to the Living Spirit Almighty within you and open your mind and heart and daily affirm, 'God is and His Presence flows through me as harmony, beauty, love, peace, joy and abundance. God watches over me and I am always surrounded by the sacred circle of God's love,' and when you give complete allegiance, loyalty and confidence to the One Power within, you are called Israel in the Bible. The Bible says:

> *Surely there is no enchantment against Jacob, neither is there any divination against Israel...* Numbers 23:23

A man who recognises the supremacy of the Spirit and the power of his own thought will find that all his ways are pleasantness and all his paths are peace.

POINTS TO REMEMBER...

1. The greatest secret of the ages is the realisation that God is One and Indivisible, the only Presence and Power, Cause and Substance. The enlightenment of man gives all power, allegiance and loyalty to the Supreme Cause (Spirit) and not to created things. You give no power to any man, stick, stone, condition, sun, moon or stars. You give power only to the Creator.
2. When we were children, we thought in images and mental pictures; consequently, the childish mind projected images of God as an old man with a beard sitting on a throne and angels with harps playing music. Childish minds pictured a devil with hoofs and horns with a tail that could sting, all of which were thought images created in our own minds based on the superstitious suggestions of adults.
3. Primitive man attributed pleasure to the gods and pain and suffering to evil powers. He supplicated the intelligences of the winds, the stars and the waters, hoping they would hear him and answer. A belief in two powers (good and evil) is a throw-back to these age-old superstitious beliefs.
4. The forces of nature are not evil; it depends upon how you use them. You can use electricity to vacuum the floor or electrocute someone. Good and evil are in man's motivation, in his thought-life.
5. Once you admit that there is any Power outside yourself, however beneficial you may conceive it to be, you have sown the seed which must sooner or later bear the fruit of 'fear,' which is the entire ruin of life, love and liberty.
6. The voodoo or witch doctor has no power but when he

wishes to impose a curse or a death prayer on an unsophisticated native, he lets the native know that he is cursed and he, believing in this power, succumbs to the suggestion, which becomes a movement of his own thought. These same curses imposed on missionaries are ridiculed by them, for they realise that evil curses have no power. There is nothing in their subconscious that accepts the negative suggestions of the witch doctor. There must be a kindred spirit or feeling in your subconscious mind before you can accept evil suggestions. How far would you get suggesting failure to a man who is full of confidence and faith in success? He would laugh at you.

7. It is foolish to give power to others when they tell you they are praying against you. The best procedure is to laugh at them, for they have none of the power they think they have. The power is of God and It is the great affirmative. It is the All-Wise One, the Mighty God, the Father of All. It moves as harmony – nothing can oppose It, thwart It or vitiate It. It is Omnipotent. Join up with It and when your thoughts are God's thoughts, God's power is with your thoughts of good. The negative thoughts of others have no power to reach you if you refuse to accept them and they will return to their point of origin with double force.
8. When God's Love unites the wife and the husband, no person can break it up. God is Love – when someone says that he is going to break up a marriage, bless him and walk on. Give power to God – no one else.
9. Hatred, resentment, jealousy and hostility kill love, peace, harmony, beauty, joy and discernment. To continue generating negative emotions is highly destructive and can end in fatal disease, acute mental aberrations or insanity.
10. Moses taught the oneness of the Spiritual Power. The Egyptian priests believed in many gods and evil powers. Moses knew the Power was One and scattered their negative thoughts like

chaff in the wind.

11. Become a straight-line thinker and give all power, recognition and loyalty to the One Supreme Power: the Living Spirit Almighty within you. Align yourself with It and let this Presence flow through you as harmony, health, peace, joy and love. You will find that all your ways are pleasantness while all your paths are peace.

3

HOW TO LET TELEPSYCHICS WORK WONDERS FOR YOU

Ralph Waldo Emerson stated, 'The finite alone has wrought and suffered. The Infinite lies stretched in smiling repose.' The law of your mind is no respecter of persons. The law indicates that what you think, you create; what you feel, you attract – what you imagine, you become. All laws are impersonal and are no respecter of persons. This truth applies to your own mind. It is dangerous to meddle with forces you do not understand. For example, if you do not learn the laws of electricity regarding its conductivity, insulation and the fact that it flows from a higher to a lower potential, you could easily electrocute yourself.

Action and reaction are universal characteristics throughout all nature. Another way of illustrating this is to point out that any thought you feel as true is impressed upon your subconscious mind (the law) and your subconscious in turn expresses whatever is impressed upon it – good, bad or indifferent.

How a man reclaimed lost love

A man once complained to me that after fifteen years of married life, he had discovered that his wife was unfaithful. She had found someone else. In talking over his problems, he mentioned that, six months before, he had visited her at the office where she worked. He noticed that her boss was very handsome and attractive, as well as wealthy. He said, 'I felt sure she would run around with him and it was my constant fear, though I said nothing to her.' At that moment, apparently, the pangs of jealousy seized him and what he feared most came upon him.

He had a knowledge of the laws of mind, having read *Amazing Laws of Cosmic Mind Power.** We discussed and elaborated on what he was doing and he understood that his constant thoughts and mental imagery of his wife's wandering had been conveyed subconsciously to his wife and were impressed into her subconscious mind. His wife knew nothing about the workings of his mind. Actually, his fear thoughts, plus his definite belief that she would run around, were picked up by her deeper mind. According to his belief, his thoughts became a near reality.

Actually, he was responsible, because the intensity of his thoughts and mental imagery were so powerful that he actually accelerated and precipitated his unfortunate marital strife. He realised his own fault. He had used the law of his mind in a very negative way. As a result, he experienced the corresponding results. Consequently, at my suggestion, he became humble enough to talk over the matter with his wife and at the same time told her the way in which he had been misusing his mind. She tearfully admitted the growing friendship and broke off the relationship with her boss. She secured another position and the spirit of forgiveness and Divine love united them again.

He banished all fear as well as his sense of jealousy by adhering to the following scientific prayer process:

My wife is receptive to my constructive thought and imagery.

---

*Dr Joseph Murphy, *Amazing Laws of Cosmic Mind Power* (Parker Publishing Company, West Nyack, New York, 1965.)

At the centre of her being is peace. God is guiding her. Divine right action governs her. There are harmony, love, peace and understanding between us. Whenever I think of her, I will immediately pronounce a benediction and say, 'God loves you and cares for you.'

He made a habit of this prayer and is now free from fear and jealousy, which are children of fear. Their marriage is growing more blessed every day. Job said, 'That which I greatly feared has come upon me.' Reverse it and it is equally true: 'That which I greatly love has come into my life and experience.'

The infinite power worked wonders for her

The title of this chapter is a result of a consultation I had with a young student from the University of Southern California. She had been studying *Psychic Perception: The Magic of Extrasensory Power** and had read about the wonderful experiences people have had in their dreams and visions of the night. She had said, I'm twenty-one years old and I have decided to get married. About a week ago I had a dialogue with my Higher-Self and this is what I said:

'You are all-wise; you know everything. Bring into my life a man who harmonises with me perfectly and who is right for me. Now I go off into the deep of sleep.'

This was her simple prayer technique. In her dream she saw a young man about her age – tall and handsome, with books under his arm. She knew immediately that he was the man she would marry. Although she had no idea who he was or where she would meet him, she was completely at peace about it. In fact, she had no further desire to pray about companionship.

About two months after her dream, she went to a religious service and the young man who sat next to her was the man she had seen in her dream two months before. He had a book under

---

*Dr Joseph Murphy, *Psychic Perception: The Magic of Extrasensory Power*

his arm – a Bible. A month later they were married.

Dreams, like this one, that envisage a future husband or wife ahead of time are not uncommon. This young student knew the laws of her mind. She was also aware that the last waking concept one has before going to sleep is etched into the subconscious mind and the latter determines how it is to come to pass. At times, it dramatises the experience when the conscious and subconscious are creatively joined in sleep.

God giveth his beloved in sleep. – Psalm 127:2

He believed the 'cards were stacked' against his success

On a recent trip to Ireland, I visited a distant cousin of mine who lives near Killarney. During dinner in his home, he kept harping on the fact that there seemed to be some sort of a 'jinx' following him. A fortune-teller had actually read the cards to observe that there were evil forces working against him, which frightened him all the more. He seemed to be under a hypnotic spell or fixed sentence by which the order of things is presented like the stacking of a deck of cards. This relative of mine is well-educated, with a degree in agriculture.

He said he had read Emerson in college but apparently had never come across Emerson's definition of fate: He (*man*) thinks his fate alien because the copula (*link* or *connection*) is hidden. But the soul (*subconscious mind*) contains the event that shall befall it, for the event is only the actualisation of its thoughts and what we pray for is always granted. The event is the print of your form. It fits you like your skin.*

I explained to him that what Ralph Waldo Emerson said is as true as are the laws of agriculture, which he had studied. It is true his conditioning, theological beliefs, emotional acceptance, thoughts and feelings determine all conditions, experiences and

---

*italics are the author's.

events in his life. In other words, the cause was in his own thought-life and not of an external nature. He began to be receptive to the truth that his subconscious mind is always reproducing his habitual thinking and beliefs. He realised that if he accepted the negative suggestions of the fortune teller, it was nevertheless a movement of his own thought –creating experiences according to his habitual thinking, in the same manner as seeds grow after their kind.

He had complete power to reject what the card reader said and to know and believe that he creates his own future through his own thinking. This is based on the age-old truth that man is what he thinks all day long.

I elaborated on the fact that, after all, the card reader had no power and did not control his life and that in a passive, psychic state, if she is very sensitive, she could tap his subconscious mind and reveal to him his present state of mind. I told him that he had the power to change his subconscious by thinking along spiritual lines and identifying with the eternal verities.

The thing which I greatly feared is come upon me Job 3:25

Actually, all the reverses, disappointments and set-backs were created by himself. He reversed his mental attitude. I wrote out a prayer for him to use night and morning, with specific instructions that he was not to subsequently deny what he affirmed:

Today is God's day. I choose happiness, success, prosperity and peace of mind. I am Divinely guided all day long and whatever I do will prosper. Whenever my attention wanders away from my thoughts of success, peace, prosperity or my good, I will immediately bring back my thoughts to the contemplation of God and His love, knowing that He careth for me.

I am a spiritual magnet, attracting to myself customers and clients who want what I have to offer. I give better service every day. I am an outstanding success in all my undertakings. I bless and prosper all those who come into my shop and also into my life. All these thoughts are now sinking into my subconscious mind and they come forth as abundance, security and peace of mind. It is wonderful!

His new attitude and constant realisation of the above truths have transformed his whole life.

She said: 'This is my seventh divorce! What am I doing wrong?'

A middle-aged woman, apparently highly agitated and in an emotionally wracked condition, asked me to throw some light on her past marriages, all of which turned out disastrously. It was easy to see that she was actually married to the same man, only each time the man had a different name and each one was progressively worse than the previous one.

I explained to her that she doesn't get what she wants in life but that she gets what she contemplates and that it is absolutely essential for her to establish the mental equivalent in her subconscious mind of what she wants before she can receive it.

Her trouble was that she was resenting the first husband, who had lied, stolen her money and jewels to then disappear. Having failed to release him, the psychic wound or festering sore was in her subconscious mind, which was the reason she attracted the second husband, the third etc. Nourishing her resentment and anger towards each successive husband, her thoughts magnified these negative emotions in her own subconscious while she attracted the image and likeness of her dominant state of mind. The subconscious always magnifies and multiplies that to which we give attention – good or bad.

I thereupon emphasised the law of mind to point out that the law is absolutely just and eminently fair in its manifestations, e.g., it is the nature of an apple seed to bring forth an apple tree; likewise, it is the law of life that she invariably and inevitably reproduces in all phases of her life – the exact duplicate of her inner nature. 'As within, so without. As in heaven (mind), so on earth (body, circumstances, conditions, experiences and events).'

I believe I cleared up the obscurities in her mind through clarification of the workings of her thought and emotions. She began to perceive that it is impossible for her to think, feel and believe one thing and then to experience something other than what she thinks, fears and expects. The law of mind is considered good and very good, because all your experiences dovetail and correlate with your inner attitudes and beliefs.

She said, 'I see now my resentment, anger and hostility toward my husbands and my failure to forgive was the reason I attracted similar types of men into my life. I must change myself. I know I have been accusing my present husband falsely and even though he is an alcoholic and a gambler, I know my imputation of his infidelity, spying on me and recriminations are projections of my own guilt, fear and insecurity.

Getting both of them together, they agreed that they wanted to make a 'go' of the marriage. She realised by the divorce – she would repeat the same pattern of accusation, self-pity, depression and suppressed rage. He decided to give up alcohol and gambling and they agreed to salute the Divinity in each other. The husband realised that a man who loves a woman doesn't do anything unloving while the wife realised that a woman is behind every successful man.

They decided to pray together and for each other morning and night, knowing that it is impossible to resent, hate or have ill will toward a person for whom we pray. The joint prayer, affirmed alternately at night and in the morning by each one, was as follows:

We know we can't have thoughts of love and resentment at the same time, for our minds can't think of two things at the same time. Whenever we think of each other we will state positively: 'God's love fills his/her soul.' We radiate love, peace, joy and goodwill toward each other. We are Divinely guided in all ways and we exalt God in each other. Our marriage is a spiritual union. We forgive ourselves for harbouring ill will, resentment and negative thoughts and resolve not to do this anymore. We know that all we have to do is to forgive ourselves and we are forgiven, as Life or God, never punishes; we do this to ourselves. Only that which belongs to love, truth and wholeness can enter our experiences.

By making a habit of this prayer, a spiritual transformation took place. They have both discovered that love dissolves everything unlike itself. Each one discovered that there is no one to change but himself.

By contemplating the truths of God and radiating love and goodwill to all, your whole world will magically melt into the image and likeness of your contemplation and your desert will rejoice and blossom as the rose. This, indeed, is letting Infinite Power work wonders for you.

POINTS TO REMEMBER...

1. The law of your mind is no respecter of persons. The law indicates that what you think, you create; what you feel, you attract – what you imagine, you become.
2. Action and reaction are universal characteristics throughout all nature. Your thought is incipient action. There is a corresponding reaction from your subconscious, based on the nature of your thought.
3. When a man believes, pictures and constantly fears that his wife will go astray, his constant thinking and imagery is conveyed to her subconscious mind and she may well do what he fears and believes she will do. This is true particularly if she does not know the laws of mind and is not 'prayed up.'
4. You banish fear and jealousy by identifying with the God-Presence in yourself and in the other person and by wishing for the other all the blessings of life, realising the ship that comes home to your brother comes home to you. The other's

success is your success; the other's good fortune is your good fortune. Love is the fulfilling of the law of health, happiness and peace of mind.

5. It is possible to see your future spouse in a dream or vision of the night. Often times your subconscious will reveal the person to you. When it actually happens, you have an intuitive feeling that your prayer is answered. You subsequently find that your future husband or wife corresponds exactly to the picture in your dreams.
6. If a man believes the cards are stacked against him or if he accepts the negative predictions of a card reader, his subconscious responds according to the nature of his belief. In fact, he is the cause of his own misfortune or so-called jinx because the postulates of his mind determine his future. He has the power to completely reject all negative suggestions. It also possible to look upon God as his silent partner, guiding, directing and prospering him in all ways. According to his belief in good fortune – good will happen to him. Man's subconscious is always reproducing his habitual thinking and imagery.
7. When a woman is deeply resentful, angry and full of ill will toward a former husband, this attitude of mind tends to attract an emotionally disturbed man possessing characteristics similar to those of the former husband. Like attracts like as 'birds of a feather flock together'. It is necessary to completely release her ex-husband, wishing for him all the blessings of life. As she makes a habit of this, she will meet him in her mind and be at peace. There is no sting where true forgiveness reigns. After forgiveness, she may then claim that the Infinite Presence and Power attracts to her a man who harmonises with her perfectly. It will then be the law of her own subconscious that will respond.
8. It takes two to make a 'go' of marriage. When each one comes to a decision to begin to exalt God within oneself and

also the other partner, the marriage will grow more blessed through the years. By contemplating the truths of God and recognising His Love in each other, the desert of their lives will rejoice and blossom as the rose.

4

HOW TELEPSYCHICS ENABLES YOU TO FORESEE THE FUTURE AND RECOGNISE THE VOICE OF INTUITION

Many people in the financial world have the capacity to anticipate the rise and fall of stocks before they occur on the objective plane of life. The reason for this is rather simple. You will always receive intuitive or inner promptings regarding the subject to which you direct your attention. Your subconscious always responds according to the nature of your concentrated thought.

A young businessman practiced telepsychics to make a small fortune

Recently, I had a conversation with a pharmacist who told me that a few years earlier he had made a study of the gold stocks in Africa, Mexico, Canada and our own country. He focussed his attention on about five stocks, which at that time were very depressed in price on the stock exchange. His telepsychic (communicating with the infinite intelligence of his subconscious mind) approach was as follows:

Every night before he went off to the deep of sleep, he would quietly say to his deeper self: Reveal to me the best investment in these gold stocks and I will be aware of the answers clearly and distinctly. The answers will come into my conscious, reasoning mind. It will be impossible for me to miss the response.

He followed the above technique regularly every night, while at the same time studying the financial background and prospects of the individual gold stocks in question. One night a man appeared to him in a dream. With a pointer, he showed him a chart with the names of the particular gold stocks, revealing their present price and future heights. He bought the stocks immediately on awakening; later on they reached the prices that he had seen in his sleep. He then sold the stocks and made a small fortune, which he said he would never have made working as a pharmacist.

He has since repurchased many of these stocks at a lower price to make considerably more money. The man appearing in his dream was a dramatisation of his subconscious mind, revealing to him clearly and distinctly the answer to his question.

How telepsychics solved a secretary's problem

Some months ago, I had a consultation with a young woman whose father had died. She was the only child whose mother had passed on when she was quite young. When she was about eight years old, her father took her to Hawaii, where they visited all the islands. He told her that he had purchased three plots of land that some day she would inherit – as he had bought them just for her. However, she could find no trace of a deed or record of any kind among the papers and did not even know which island he had referred to, since he had never mentioned the matter again.

I suggested to her that she relax at night – quiet her mind. It was necessary to imagine she was talking to the Infinite Spirit within her. I urged her to conduct a dialogue with this Presence and explained to her that this process is called telepsychics and that she would get a definite response. The prerequisites were sincerity, recognition and acceptance of the answer.

Accordingly, she conducted an imaginary conversation with her Higher Self along these lines:

My father's deed and the transaction regarding the property are somewhere and I know that you, my Higher Self, knows and I accept the answer now. I give thanks for the answer and it is so.

She then quietly lulled herself to sleep with the one word, 'answer' repeating it over and over again.

The last waking concept with which you go to sleep every night is etched into your subconscious. If your idea is sufficiently emotionalised with faith and confidence, your subconscious will determine how the answer will come, as it knows only the answer.

She repeated the above-mentioned technique every night for about two weeks and at the end of that time, she said her Dad appeared to her in her sleep. He was smiling and said:

I'm going to unravel your problem. The deed and sales contract are in the family Bible, the one your grandmother used to read. Look at Page 150 and you will find it in a small envelope. I must go now but I'll see you again. It's your Daddy – don't think it's a dream.

She awoke somewhat shaken and rushed downstairs and opened the Bible. There were the papers she was looking for: tax receipts, sales records and deed. Thus, her dream saved her much time and expense.

No one knows exactly what method the subconscious mind will use in answering your prayer. The capacity of clairvoyance is one of its powers; thus, the secretary could, by means of clairvoyance, see the location of the deed. Her subconscious could weave it into a dream image, showing her father revealing the answer to her, somewhat similar to a writer of a play who formulates the words uttered by his characters.

If you say it was actually the 'spirit' of her father, this belief would be accepted by many, as this young woman believed implicitly that it was her father. We must remember that there is telepathic communication every day among loved ones: fathers, mothers, sons, daughters, relatives, friends, etc., all of whom are very much alive on their plane. There is no death and all our loved ones are around us, separated by frequency only. They each have subjective minds like all of us and have rarefied, attenuated bodies capable of penetrating closed doors and collapsing time and space.

To say that your father or mother could not possibly send you a telepathic message from the next dimension would be like saying your father could not send you a telepathic message from Boston or that he couldn't phone you or wire you a message. We are all in the one mind, common to all individual persons. Every person is an inlet and an outlet to that one universal mind.

Mind and Spirit, which is the reality of all of us, can't die; for God is Life (Spirit) and that is our life now. God is Spirit and the Living Spirit Almighty indwells you, walks and talks in you. Thousands of years ago, the ancient Hindu mystics said:

You (Spirit) were never born; you (Spirit) will never die; water wets you not; fire burns you not; swords pierce you not; and wind blows you not away.

A Frequently Asked Question

'Do disembodied spirits (those loved ones living in the next dimensions and possessing fourth-dimensional bodies) communicate with the living?'

My answer to this is that we are still talking about embodied spirits, whether on this three-dimensional plane or the next fourth-dimensional plane. Dr Rhine and many other scientists have demonstrated experimentally, beyond a shadow of a doubt, that telepathic communication exists between embodied spirits here. Of course, that means you and your friends or loved ones. Your loved ones in the next dimension are embodied spirits also and are as much alive as you are.

Telepsychics and Extrasensory Travel

Many people, consciously and unconsciously, have found themselves outside their natural bodies and have discovered that they have another body, sometimes called the subtle body, astral body, fourth-dimensional body etc. It is a body with a higher molecular vibration, somewhat like a fan that oscillates at such a high speed that the blades become invisible.

It is well-known in academic and scientific circles that man is comprised of much more than his body. It has been demonstrated that man can see, hear and engage in extrasensory travel completely independent of his physical being. The late Dr Hornell Hart, an associate of Dr Rhine's at Duke University, did considerable research on 'man outside his body'. He suggested further experimentation and investigation.

You will find very interesting and unique experiences in *Infinite Power for Richer Living** and in *Psychic Perception: The Magic of Extrasensory Power*** about men and women in everyday life who have projected their bodies thousands of miles and then were able to report what they had seen and witnessed.

How telepsychics won him $100,000 in one day

Some months ago, I spoke at the Church of Religious Science in Las Vegas, Nevada, at the request of Dr David Howe, the minister in charge. One of the men who attended the lecture visited me at my hotel for advice regarding a domestic problem.

---

*Dr Joseph Murphy, *Infinite Power for Richer Living* (Parker Publishing Company, West Nyack, New York, 1969.)

**Dr Joseph Murphy, *Psychic Perception: The Magic of Extrasensory Power* (Parker Publishing Company, Inc., West Nyack, New York, 1971.)

During the course of the conversation, he said that he was a bookie and handled large sums of money on horse-betting throughout the country. He said that he protects himself from large losses by using his subconscious mind regularly and systematically. When he receives too much money on one or two horses, he tries to lay some of it off with other bookies but every night he studies the race-sheet diligently, limiting his interests to two particular horses that he favours; then he says to his subconscious: 'I am turning this request over to you. Reveal to me the winners in the first or third race (or whatever two races he favours)'; then he falls off to sleep with the words 'winners, winners, winners.'

At sleep time the conscious mind is creatively joined to the subconscious and the latter accepts the last waking concept and proceeds to answer him in its own way. Often times he sees the race and the winner while sound asleep in the bed. Other times he sees the race in his dream but forgets the winner when he awakens. One night he saw 'Look-Me-Over' win the race and the odds were close to 27–1 for first place. He bet $4,000 and won about $100,000.

You will notice that this dream was of a precognitive nature, i.e., he saw the results of the race 24 hours before it occurred on the race track but it was definitely connected with his job as a bookie. Your subconscious mind is impersonal and no respecter of persons. It will give intuition to the banker, relative to money; to the doctor, relative to healing; to the chemist, relative to chemical formulas; to the stockbroker, relative to investments; and the inventor, interested in a new discovery, may receive the entire design in his dream. Your subconscious will give you promptings, ideas, answers as also definite intuitive impressions based on the nature of your focussed attention and intense interest.

[§]Before 1973

How to Remember a Special Dream

I explained to this bookie how to recapture the memory of his special dream about a winner, which had eluded him. I suggested that whenever he awakens in the morning, the very first thing he should say to himself is, 'I remember,' then the dream will come back in full form. (He has tried it and it works.)

Telepsychics in the life of Luther Burbank

The name of Luther Burbank is familiar to all and according to his own statement, it was a common practice for him to send a telepathic message to his sister whenever he wanted her to accompany him to visit their ailing mother. On these occasions he never had to resort to the telephone or telegraph service.

Dr Phineas Parkhurst Quimby could appear at a distance

Dr Quimby, undoubtedly the foremost spiritual healer in America, has been known to have stated: 'I know that I can condense my identity and appear also at a distance.' His astral or fourth-dimensional body was as real to Quimby as was his physical body. These appearances of Quimby to patients 100 or more miles away from his home took place beginning about 1845 or 1846.

Quimby demonstrated that man is a transcendental being and is not bound by time, space and matter. To cite one instance in the extraordinary life of this unique spiritual healer:

He wrote to a woman who lived a great distance from his home in Belfast, Maine, stating that he would visit her on a certain day, although he never revealed the exact time. Due to an oversight, the letter was never mailed. However, while the woman for whom he promised to pray and visit was entertaining another woman at dinner, the guest said, 'There is a man standing behind your chair,' and she described him in detail. The lady of the house declared, 'Oh, that is Dr Quimby. He is treating me.' Dr Quimby was mentally and spiritually present with her, wearing a fourth-dimensional or subtle body, which was seen by the guest in the home.

Physically, Quimby was in his home in Belfast at that time, concentrating on his patient and contemplating the Divine ideal – the healing, purifying force of the Infinite Healing Presence flowing through his patient – and he decided at the same time to project himself into her presence, undoubtedly with the idea of instilling greater faith and receptivity in his patient.

Telepsychics enabled a young man to win a scholarship and a new car

Robert Wright, 19 years of age, assists me every Saturday morning in putting together my radio program in a soundproof room in my home. He has been practising the law of his mind every night before retiring by quietly exclaiming the following:

Infinite intelligence in my subconscious mind guides me in all my studies in college and reveals to me all the answers. I am always poised, serene and calm. This is why I pass all my examinations in Divine order. I know a car is an idea in the Universal Mind. I claim a new car now, which comes to me in Divine order. I give thanks for the answered prayer. I know that the nature of my deeper mind is to respond to my requests and I also know that my idea, when repeated faithfully, will be etched in my subconscious and come to pass.

The sequel was interesting. He experienced a pre vision one night about a week prior to a special examination and saw all the questions to be asked in a dream. He subsequently got excellent marks and won a scholarship for a considerable sum of money, which will aid him in his education. The car he was driving to college broke down on the freeway and the same day, he was presented with a gift of a new station wagon.

When the car broke down, he affirmed boldly: 'Only good can come out of this,' and only good came to him. The key to a full and happy life is to rejoice in the goodness of God in the land of the living.

POINTS TO REMEMBER...

1. You will always receive intuition from your subconscious based on the subject to which you are attentive. For example, if you give attention to the study of a particular stock or stocks, you may receive an inner prompting, a hunch or predominant feeling to purchase a certain stock; or you may, as one man did, see in your dream the name of the stock and the future height of the stock. Your subconscious dramatises the answer in ways you do not know. You must be on the alert, on the *qui vive*, so to speak, to take advantage of the answer.
2. If you are looking for lost or mislaid items, turn your request over to your subconscious mind, claiming that the supreme intelligence in your subconscious knows the answer and will reveal it to you. Trust your deeper mind, which knows all and sees all. In one instance, a girl reported that her father appeared to her in a dream and told her to look in a certain page of the family Bible. It was there she found all the papers she needed to claim her property. The ways of your subconscious are beyond finding out.
3. Within your subconscious are the faculties of clairvoyance, clairaudience and other supernormal faculties. This is co-extensive with all wisdom and power. Within your subconscious are all the powers of the Infinite Being, which can fetch wisdom from afar, pick the brain of the other or read the contents of a closed safe. Turn your requests over to It with faith and confidence and expect an answer. As sure as the sun rises in the morning, so will there be a resurrection of your desire.
4. You are mind and Spirit; you are immortal. God is Spirit and that Spirit is the Life Principle within you – the Reality of

you. Spirit was never born and will never die. Your journey is ever onward, upward and God-ward. There is no end to the glory, which is man. Never in all eternity could you exhaust the wonders and glories of the Infinite.

5. Loved ones on this plane communicate telepathically with each other. It would be foolish to say that the same loved ones who go to the next dimension of life, which is all around us and interpenetrates this plane, could not communicate with us. The same Spirit and Mind are in them that are in you, as well. There is no separation in the One Mind. I believe definitely there are many instances where you receive definite, concrete messages from loved ones in the next dimension of life. There is no death – it is foolish to talk about messages from the dead. All those who ever lived are living now. Even a million or billion years from now, you will also be alive, revealing more and more of the qualities, attributes and wonders of the Infinite.
6. It is well known in academic and scientific circles that man can think, see, feel, hear and travel independent of his physical being. Astral travel or that which is called extrasensory travel, has been known for ages. Many have had out-of-the-body experiences unconsciously; others have experimented in astral travel by concentrating on visiting a friend or sick relative. They found themselves by the bedside, possessing visual, auditory and tactile capacities. They are not ghosts or apparitions; they merely have clothed themselves with a subtle body which is rarefied and attenuated, capable of passing through closed doors and transcending time and space. Remember, you are a mental and spiritual being. Someday you will use all these inner faculties and powers completely independent of your present three-dimensional body.
7. A bookie who concentrates and focusses his attention on horses in a certain race prior to sleep, asking his subconscious for winners, approaches his subconscious with full recognition

of its powers plus faith and confidence and expectancy and invariably receives answers. There are many people in England who have foreseen the winner of the English Derby every year and consequently made a small fortune. I knew a Dr Green, whose hobby was horseracing and who made a quarter of a million pounds (English) due to pre-vision, seeing the result of the race for six successive years in a row.

8. When you say, 'I don't dream,' or 'I can't remember my dreams,' the moment you awaken in the morning, say to yourself quietly, 'I remember,' and the whole structure of the dream will come clearly into your conscious, reasoning mind.
9. Luther Burbank didn't bother telephoning or telegraphing his sister when he wished her to accompany him on a visit to their sick mother; instead, he sent her a telepathic message, which she invariably received and complied with.
10. Dr Phineas Parkhurst Quimby of Belfast, Maine, said in 1847: 'I know that I can condense my identity and appear at a distance.' He did this with several patients and ministered to them in his astral or fourth-dimensional body, which we all possess this very moment. Quimby demonstrated that we are transcendental beings, not governed by the factors of time, space or matter.
11. A young college student claims regularly and systematically that the infinite intelligence of his subconscious mind guides him in his studies and reveals all the answers to him. Often, his subconscious responds prior to the examinations by revealing all the questions to him on a screen in his mind. He awakens and looks up all the answers – to invariably find that the very questions appearing to him in a dream are identical with those on the examination, perhaps a week or two weeks later. This is called precognition, seeing an event before it happens. The questions were already in the Mind. He simply tuned in and picked them up. The wisdom of the subconscious mind caused the professor to ask the same questions, thinking all

the time that his conscious mind was making the decision and selecting the questions. This is why many professors do not know the cause of their actions. Indeed, the student often seems to be smarter than the teacher from a mental and spiritual standpoint.

5

HOW TELEPSYCHICS REVEALS ANSWERS IN DREAMS AND VISIONS

During a consultation some weeks ago, a man asked me: 'What are dreams and what causes me to dream?' That is a good question. I don't think one can give a simple answer to this question. Dreams have been discussed and interpreted in the various Bibles of the world and among all races and nations, because dreams are of a universal nature.

Dreams are dramatisations of the subconscious mind of man. For this reason, they are very personal. All men and women in the world, as well as animals, dream. When you think about it, about one-third of your life is spent in sleep. While sleeping, your dream life is active to a great extent. Many scientific and academic laboratories are engaged in the study of sleep and dreams and they often reveal amazing results.

The Power of Suggestion

Many years ago in New York, I witnessed a psychologist from Berlin as he hypnotised some students in his home. He suggested that one would dream about marriage, a church service and a honeymoon; to another it was suggested that he would dream of India and its holy temples; to another, that he would dream that he was a millionaire etc. He suggested that each would recall his dream but would have no conscious memory of what was suggested to him.

After about ten minutes, all the subjects were awakened and recalled their dreams promptly. All the dreams corresponded accurately with the nature of the suggestion. The reason for this is that the subconscious is amenable to suggestions and reasoning deductively only, reacts according to the nature of the suggestion.

Undoubtedly, many of your dreams are due to your habitual thinking during the day, as well as to your reactions to the day's events, all of which are impressed on your subconscious mind. Your deeper mind elaborates, activates and magnifies whatever you deposit in it.

Most people are very familiar with the names of Sigmund Freud, who wrote the *Interpretation of Dreams* in 1899, Carl Jung and Alfred Adler, all of whom have written extensively about the subconscious and the dream lives of their patients. Each of the men varies in his interpretation of dreams and the inner urges and drives in man; consequently, they have evolved different schools of psychology, namely *psychoanalysis* (Freud), *analytical psychology* (Jung) and *individual psychology* (Adler). The differences between these men in the interpretation of dreams and the approach to the subconscious are rather conflicting. However, it is not the purpose of this book to elucidate them here. Nevertheless, a discussion of dreams will serve to show you that the key to solving many of your problems often comes as a clear-cut, definite answer in a dream.

How a school teacher solved her problems through a dream

While holding a consultation with a young schoolteacher, she mentioned that she was frightfully frustrated in the teaching field, that she had never liked it but that her parents had more or less coerced her into entering the profession.

I suggested to her that her subconscious mind knows all about her hidden talents and that if she contacted the infinite intelligence in her deeper mind, she would get a response. The technique she used, at my suggestion, was to say to herself prior to retiring:

Infinite Intelligence reveals to me my true place in life, where I am expressing myself at the highest level. I have a wonderful income consistent with integrity and honesty. I accept the answer now and I sleep in peace.

The first night following this meditation, she had a very vivid dream. She felt herself to be in a very large building where she saw a man pointed to a certain door, suggesting that she go through that door. As she entered the room, she observed the walls, which were full of beautiful paintings. As she looked at them, she found herself fascinated, absorbed, in a way, transfixed. In her dream, she said to herself, 'This is it,' which meant she had found her true place in life.

She phoned me to say she was taking up painting and planned to resign her teaching position, which she did. Almost immediately she fell in love with painting, her hidden talent was revealed to her. Now she is extremely successful. Recently I bought one of her beautiful paintings for $200[§]. Her first exhibit held in her home for a group of friends and former teachers netted $2,500 in sales.

Her favourite Biblical quotation is:

I set before thee an open door which no man can shut.

– Revelations 3:8

[§]Before 1973

There is no obstacle to the unfolding of your heart's dream unless you place the impediment, the difficulty, the delay or the obstruction in your conscious mind. There is nothing to oppose the omnipotent power and wisdom of your deeper mind.

One of this young artist's paintings captivated one of her former professors, who eventually married her. He now has a special assignment in Australia and they are both following the release of their hidden talents in that country and are very happy. Her subconscious magnified her good exceedingly.

How Telepsychics Lifted Her Burden

Recently, one of my radio listeners phoned me and said that her father had passed on about a week before. She explained that she knew her father always kept large sums of money in the house, as it was his custom to fly to Las Vegas twice a month where he spent the weekends at the roulette wheel and was, as she said, extraordinarily lucky. He had told his daughter that he only played when he had that inner feeling or hunch that he would win and the moment that inner monitor or intuition left him, he would stop playing immediately.

His transition was rather sudden; he passed away in his sleep. She had searched everywhere she could think of for the money she felt was hidden nearby but to no avail.

I suggested to her that she talk to her subconscious mind and undoubtedly, she would get the answer. I explained to her that when she quieted her conscious mind and when she was relaxed and at ease, the wisdom of her subconscious would rise to the surface mind and reveal the answer.

She read the 23rd Psalm over and over for about ten minutes and then closed her eyes, relaxed and let go, quietly claiming that the wisdom of her subconscious would reveal where her father's money was located and that she would recognise the answer when it came. She fell asleep in the chair. Suddenly, she said,

'Daddy came to me,' and he appeared by the chair and smiled. He seemed so real and natural she could hardly believe it was he. He said, 'Elizabeth, the money is in a steel box in the cellar behind a box of tools and the key is in the drawer where I keep my correspondence.'

She awakened immediately and to her surprise and delight, she found $13,000 in denominations of $50 and $100 bills. Her joy was twofold. She was delighted to find the money, which she needed badly. But more than that, she had that inner conviction and silent knowing that her father was still watching over her.

No one can disprove immortality. The Bible says:

> *And this is life eternal, that they might know thee the only true God* – John 17:3

How to Let Telepsychics Give You the Answer You Need

One of the best times for tapping the wisdom of your subconscious mind* for ideas, answers and inspiration is prior to sleep. The reason for this is, generally speaking, you are more relaxed, at ease and you are ready for quietude and deep sleep. Quiet your mind by repeating a few verses of the 23rd Psalm and let go.

For example, if you are a sales manager and you plan to speak to the salesmen the next day, you may say:

I know the infinite intelligence of my subconscious mind will guide and direct my talk tomorrow and reveal the right words to me that will inspire, lift up and stimulate all these men. Whatever I say will be right for the occasion and all will be blessed and benefited.

Speak these words silently or audibly, whichever you choose. Do this with faith and confidence that your subconscious will

*Dr Joseph Murphy, *The Power of Your Subconscious Mind* (Prentice-Hall, Inc., Englewood Cliffs, NJ, 1963.)

answer you. It never fails.

In the beginning, if you know a week in advance that you are to speak to a group, pray about it every night and you will find that, even though you may have an outline of your talk prepared, ideas will spontaneously flash into your conscious mind while you are talking and you will discover that these words are right for the occasion.

SHOULD I ACCEPT THAT POSITION?

In asking that question, do not permit your conscious mind to dictate the answer. It is all right to look at the pros and cons of the situation. Once you have done this and are still not quite sure that you should accept the position, just turn your request over to your subconscious as follows:

I know my subconscious is all wise. It is interested in my welfare and it reveals to me the answer about the position. I follow the lead which comes to me. Then lull yourself to sleep with the one word, 'Answer.'

Knowing that your subconscious is responsive to you, do this with complete faith that you will receive the answer and that it will be right for you. It may come as a flash to you in the morning when you awaken or in a vivid dream wherein you will have that inner feeling that it is right for you.

In applying the above technique, you can learn to apply the same process during waking hours with the same success. Quiet your mind, be alone, close your eyes, cleanse your conscious mind by thinking of the boundless wisdom and the infinite power of your deeper mind which knows all and sees all. Think of nothing but the question you are asking. Continue doing this for a few minutes in a quiet, passive and receptive way.

When the answer does not well up immediately from your deeper mind, stop pondering to go on about your usual work. Let your request gestate in the darkness of your subconscious mind and the moment you least expect it, the answer will pop into your conscious mind just as toast pops out of the toaster.

The Dream Is Its Own Interpretation

Your dream is personal to you and the same symbols that you receive, when they appear in someone else's mind, may have an entirely different meaning. Your subconscious speaks to you symbolically in dreams. An ancient Hebrew mystic said that at night the wife (the *subconscious*) talks back to her husband (*conscious* mind) and sometimes tells him in no uncertain terms that he has been polluting her with negative thoughts, fears and destructive emotions.

How telepsychics warned her and she cancelled her wedding plans

A young woman – who was engaged to a man she had promised to marry – came to me for consultation. She said that she didn't know why but that she was deeply troubled and felt depressed. She wanted to withdraw from the engagement but didn't want to hurt the young man's feelings.

The best time to prevent a divorce is before marriage.

During the course of our discussion, she said that she had experienced a recurrent dream for ten consecutive nights in which a man with a long beard pointed to the Star of David, a figure consisting of a six-pointed star, which serves as the symbol of Judaism.

I asked her what the dream meant to her, as the Talmud said: 'Every dream has its own interpretation.' She responded by saying that she no longer attended the synagogue. She used to read and study the Psalms of David but the man to whom she was betrothed was an atheist who ridiculed all religious beliefs.

I explained to her that the law of the subconscious is self-preservation and undoubtedly it was trying to protect her by the symbolic dramatisation of the Star of David and that her own intuition would reveal the correctness of the interpretation, as the symbol had to ring a bell in her own heart.

She broke off the engagement and the recurrent dream ceased at once. She had a profound sense of peace. She went back to the synagogue and renewed her interpretations and meditations of the Psalms of David and prayed that Infinite Intelligence would attract a man who harmonised with her in every way and who had a deep reverence for the God-Presence within all people. She has since married a rabbinical student and is quite contented.

She looked upon her recurrent dream as a warning, which undoubtedly it was. The Bible says:

> *And being warned of God in a dream that they should not return to Herod, they departed into their own country another way.* – Matthew 2:12

How telepsychics solved a man's agonising problem

A man from New York flew out to Beverly Hills to interview me. He said that he had been married for six years to a woman from Los Angeles. She had mentioned to him from time to time that she used to listen to my lectures on mental and spiritual laws. However, suddenly, about a year ago, she had disappeared from their home, leaving no note or explanation. He thought she might be a member of my organisation; however, I had no knowledge of her whereabouts, in fact her name was not on our mailing list.

He had misappropriated funds, which she had given him to the extent of $60,000. He felt guilty about it and wanted to make amends. In the meantime, he had become the heir to his mother's estate and was in a position to repay the money to his wife. He felt that to be the reason she had walked out. Detectives failed to find her and her relatives had no clue.

He said to me, 'I don't know why I came to you but I have a hunch that she might come to see you. I am leaving $10,000 with you with her name on it and if she comes, give it to her and ask her to get in touch with me; I love her and want her back.' He added, 'Be sure to tell her of my inheritance.' I promised to keep in touch with him and let him know if she contacted me.

Nothing happened as two months passed then a woman phoned from San Francisco, saying to my secretary that it was extremely urgent and important that she see me and that she was flying down to Beverly Hills that morning. I saw this woman in the evening and she unfolded a most amazing drama of the mind.

A few nights before, she said, I had appeared to her in a dream and told her that I had a sum of money for her; that all of her money that her husband had misused was waiting for her when she returned home to New York. This, she said, is why she was here. The dream, she said, was so vivid, so realistic, that it was like a vision. The room was full of light and she felt ecstatic.

She said to me, 'You read from the Bible,' and she said she heard my voice saying:

> *In a dream, in a vision of the night, when deep sleep falleth upon men, in slumberings upon the bed; then he openeth the ears of men and sealeth their instruction.*– Job 33:15, 16

I had no recollection of the woman and did not recall ever meeting her. However, one night I turned a request over to my subconscious as follows: 'Infinite Intelligence knows where Mrs X is and reveals her whereabouts to me. She contacts me in Divine order. It is God in action.'

I gave her the $10,000[§] and she flew back to New York to join her husband. She told me she had left because of his lies to her and because he had squandered all her money. She had been praying for guidance and Divine right action. Apparently my prayer was resurrected as an answer to her problems and her subconscious projected an image of the author with the message that answered her prayer.

[§]in 1973 or earlier

POINTS TO REMEMBER...

1. Dreams are dramatisations of your subconscious mind. When you are asleep, your subconscious mind is very much awake and continuously active, as it never sleeps. Your subconscious usually speaks in symbolic form. Scientific experiments show that eye movements occur when a person is dreaming. You may get answers to your problems in a dream.
2. Your subconscious mind is amenable to suggestion and responds according to the nature of the suggestion, whether true or false. For example, you can repeatedly suggest to yourself before you go to sleep that you are going to dream about the Lakes of Killarney and you will have a wonderful fictionalised dramatisation of the lakes. You will enjoy the marvellous scenery portrayed by your subconscious.
3. Freud, Adler and Jung vary in their approach to the subconscious and in their interpretations of dreams. In this book, the purpose is to show you that many people who are praying for solutions to their problems get very clear-cut answers while sound asleep, usually in symbolic form and often times in a very literal way.
4. A school teacher praying for true expression was instructed in a dream to go through a certain door. It was there she found herself in an art gallery full of beautiful paintings. Her intuition told her that this is her mission in life and she took up painting and became an immediate success.
5. A young girl could not find money hidden by her father, who had passed on suddenly. She asked her subconscious mind to reveal to her where it was and while asleep, her father appeared to her and gave her explicit instructions where to find it. The ways of the subconscious are beyond finding out. You can never tell the exact way the answer will come. All you need do is turn your request over with confidence and to trust it implicitly to give you the answer

and the moment you least expect it, the answer will come out of the blue.

6. The best time to tap the subconscious is prior to sleep, when you are relaxed, at peace and ready for quietude and deep sleep. If you are seeking an answer to some problem, talk to your subconscious and affirm that the wisdom of your subconscious knows the answer and that you have absolute faith in the answer; then lull yourself to sleep with one word, 'Answer,' and your subconscious will do the rest. You can apply the same process during waking hours by stilling your mind and perhaps, by meditating on the 23rd Psalm. Then think of the infinite intelligence and boundless wisdom within you. Think of the answer. Do this for a few minutes and let it go. The answer will probably come to you when you are preoccupied with something else.
7. If you are religiously inclined and studying spiritual subjects, your subconscious, which seeks to protect you, may present a religious symbol to you, which will have deep meaning for you. A Jewish girl about to get married had a recurrent dream (always very important) in which the Star of David appeared to her every night. Intuitively, she knew what it meant and cancelled the proposed marriage. Subsequent events confirmed the truth of the answer received in her dreams.
8. A husband sought everywhere for his wife, who had deserted him. He prayed for guidance and Divine right action and his minister prayed that the infinite intelligence of his subconscious would reveal her whereabouts that he might give her $10,000[$] left with him by her husband. The wisdom of the subconscious dramatised an image of the minister to her while she was asleep. He quoted the Bible and told her in detail about the money and how her husband wanted to

---

[$]in 1973 or earlier

make amends. She followed the dream, visited the minister and found her dream was literally true to the letter.

I the Lord (your subconscious) will make myself known unto him in a vision and will speak unto him in a dream.
– Numbers 12:6

6

EFFECTIVE TELEPSYCHIC TECHNIQUES AND PROCESSES OF PRAYER – HOW THEY WORK FOR YOU

The dictionary defines prayer as:

1. A devout petition to or any form of spiritual communion with God or in object of worship.
2. The act or practice of praying to God or an object of worship.
3. A spiritual communion with God, as a supplication, thanksgiving, adoration or confession.
4. A formula or sequence of words used in or appointed for praying, e.g., the Lord's Prayer.
5. A religious observance, either public or private, consisting wholly or mainly of prayer.
6. A petition, entreaty.

In this book you are told simply and plainly that you answer your own prayer. The reason for this is extraordinarily simple: Whatever your conscious mind really believes and accepts as true, your subconscious mind will bring forth consistently as form, function, experience and events. Your subconscious mind accepts your conviction, whether true or false, as it reasons deductively only. If you give it a false suggestion, it will assume the correctness of your premise and dramatise the result accordingly.

How Your Subconscious Mind Works

Suppose a psychologist or psychiatrist hypnotised you (in that state your conscious, reasoning mind is suspended and your subconscious* is amenable to suggestion) and then suggested to you that you were the President of the United States. Your subconscious would accept the statement as true. It does not reason, choose or differentiate as does your conscious mind. You would assume all the airs of importance and dignity that you believed to be the legitimate concomitant of that position.

If you were given a glass of water and told you were drunk, you would play the role of a drunkard to the best of your ability. If you told the psychiatrist that you were allergic to timothy grass and he placed a glass of distilled water under your nose, telling you at the same time that it was timothy grass, you would generate all the symptoms of an allergic attack and the physiological and physical reactions would be the same as if the water were actually timothy grass.

If you were told that you were a beggar, in a desparately unfortunate and difficult situation your demeanour would immediately change. You would assume a humble and meek attitude with an imaginary tin cup in your hand.

In short, you may be made to believe that you are anything, such as a statue, dog, soldier or swimmer. Then you will act the part suggested with amazing fidelity to the nature of the suggestion,

---

*Read *The Power of Your Subconscious Mind* by Dr Joseph Murphy (Prentice Hall, Inc., Englewood Cliffs, NJ, 1963)

insofar as your knowledge extends of the characteristics of the thing that is suggested. Another important point to remember is that your subconscious mind always accepts the dominant of two ideas; i.e., it accepts your conviction without question whether your premise is true or absolutely false.

Why the Scientific Thinker Does Not Beg, Beseech and Supplicate a Far Off God

The modern, scientific, straight-line thinker looks at God as the infinite intelligence within his subconscious mind. He doesn't care whether people call it the super-conscious, unconscious, subjective mind or whether they call this supreme intelligence Allah, Brahma, Jehovah, Reality or Spirit or the All-Seeing Eye.

All the powers of God are within you. God is Spirit, however and a spirit has no face, form or figure; it is timeless, spaceless and eternal. The same Spirit dwells in every man. This is why Paul says: *that thou stir up the gift of God, which is in thee* – II Timothy 1:6. You are also told *The kingdom of God is within you* – Luke 17:21.

Yes, God is in your thought, your feeling, your imagination. In other words, the invisible part of you is God. God is the Life Principle in you: boundless love, absolute harmony, infinite intelligence. Know that you can contact this invisible power through your thought; strip the whole process of prayer from mystery, superstition, doubt and wonder. The Bible tells you that the *Word was God* – John 1:1.

Your word is your thought expressed. Based on what you have already read in this chapter, every thought is creative and tends to manifest itself in your life according to the nature of your thought. It stands to reason that any time you discover the creative power, you have discovered God, as there is only one Creative Power – not two, three or 1000, just one.... *Hear, O Israel* (illumined and awakened man); *the Lord* (the Supreme

Power) *our God is one Lord* (one Power, Presence, Cause and Substance) – Mark 12:29.

Why the Scientific Thinker Never Supplicates or Petitions

We are told in a very simple, practical and down to earth manner by the wisdom of the ages from Isaiah 65:24

> *Before they call, I will answer; and while they are yet speaking, I will hear.*

This is why the straight-line thinker who knows the laws of his own mind looks upon it as absurd, foolish and silly to beg for something already given him. In other words, before you call for a solution to a problem in astrophysics, chemistry, human relations, loneliness, sickness, poverty or being lost in the jungle, the answer to any problem under the sun is awaiting you for the simple reason that the infinite intelligence of your subconscious knows only the answer to any question, regardless of its nature.

This is plain common sense or just old-fashioned horse sense. Infinite intelligence in your subconscious is all-wise, knows all and It created the universe and all things therein contained. Having created all things, including all men and the myriads of galaxies in the universe, why should any thinking being conclude that the Supreme Intelligence within his subconscious doesn't know the answer? Actually, the wisdom of your subconscious knows only the answer, as it has no problem. Just think for a moment: If Infinite Intelligence had a problem, who would solve it?

I was rescued by the guardian angel

When I was a very young boy, my mother told me that I had a special guardian angel who would always watch over me. Whenever I was in trouble the angel would come to my rescue.

Like all children, my mind was impressionable and I accepted the beliefs of my parents.

One time, accompanied by some other boys, I was completely lost in the jungle. I said to the boys that my guardian angel would lead us out and save us. Some of the boys laughed and ridiculed the idea. Several of the boys accompanied me and I had that inner feeling, a sort of predominant hunch, to go in a certain direction, where we eventually met a hunter who treated us kindly and rescued us. The other boys who refused to accompany us were never found.

There is no guardian angel with wings watching over anybody. My blind belief in a guardian angel caused my subconscious mind to respond in its own way, compelling me to go in a certain direction. My deeper mind also knew where the hunter was and directed us accordingly.

The Bible says:

> *I will set him on high, because he hath known my name. He shall call upon me and I will answer him: I will be with him in trouble* – Psalms 91:14–15

The name means the nature of that infinite intelligence in your subjective depths. The words subjective and subconscious are synonymous. The nature of infinite intelligence within you is to respond to the nature of your call.

If you are lost in the jungle and don't have a compass and have no idea where the North Star is, in other words, you have no sense of direction, remember that the creative intelligence within your subconscious made the universe and all things contained there. Surely it does not need a compass to lead you out. If you do not recognise the wisdom within you, it is just the same as if it were not there.

Suppose you brought a very primitive person into your home who had never seen a tap or an electric switch and you left him alone for a week in your house. He would die of thirst and also remain in darkness, yet all the time water and light would have been available. Millions of people throughout the world are like this primitive man. They fail to see that no matter what they seek, no matter what the problem, the answer awaits them and all they have to do is to call with faith and confidence on the wisdom of their subjective mind and the answer will come from the depths of themselves.

Experience the Riches and Rewarding Experiences of Scientific Prayer

The word 'prayer' has such a variety of meanings with such a long history that, in this book, the author feels committed to explain the process of prayer and prayer therapy in the simplest possible terms.

I talk with many people in different parts of the world who are definitely encrusted with old ideas which no up-to-date, modem high school boy could accept as true, plus old rituals and ceremonies which no intelligent man or woman could possibly believe. Do not shut yourself off from the tremendous benefits and blessings which can come to you through real prayer, by preconceptions gathered in childhood and adhered to throughout the years.

How a young man became an airline pilot

The following is taken from a letter from a young man who told me that all the odds were against him. He asked me to include his letter in this book so that it might help others. Here are his own words, which I am sure they will make sense to the attentive reader.

> This is an experience which occurred to me. Maybe you can use all or part of it to help others.
>
> I always wanted to be an Airline Pilot. Years ago I used the laws of mind to bring the time and money to me to

become trained enough and have enough experience and licenses to be an Airline Pilot. Just as I was ready to pursue the issue, our nation went into a recession. All airlines layed off many pilots. I wandered away from my daily utilisation of Truth. When our airline began calling back its pilots and looking for new ones I found myself off the Beam.

There were 2500 applicants for these 10 openings, 90% of these had more experience than I. One Sunday you stated 'You must come to a decision and claim what you want to believe.'

While driving to and from work I would visualise myself wearing the pilot's uniform and while driving to work, I would visualise myself driving to pick up a flight or attending the necessary classes. I felt I was EXPECTED at these places and I couldn't be late. The door was not closed to me, I was EXPECTED to step through it where they were waiting for me.

After 3 weeks of imagining and feeling the reality of it all, the personnel manager called me and said he wanted to interview me. The class was full but one man dropped out the day before class started. My paperwork was rushed and people were held overtime to process me. They said I was the perfect answer to their problem and they were grateful to me. Six of the above openings were scheduled to favoured sons.

This young man, about 21 years of age, realises that whatever idea he claims and feels to be true will be impressed on his subconscious and will come to pass. This is *real* prayer.

Do Not Beg a God in Space

The straight-line thinker knows that God or the creative intelligence of his subconscious mind, will respond according to his personal belief or conviction. He knows that there are laws governing the operation of the entire cosmos and that, as Emerson says, 'Nothing happens by chance. Everything is pushed from behind,' which means that if your prayer is answered, it must be answered according to the laws of your own mind, whether you are aware of it or not.

The Living Spirit within you does not suspend the laws of life to favour someone because of his or her religious affiliations or saintly character. The laws of life do not vary; neither are we dealing with a law of caprice or of favouritism, for *God is no respecter of persons*…[For God all are equal.]Acts 10:34. You are dealing with a universal law that receives the impress of your thoughts and beliefs and acts accordingly; if you impress your deeper mind negatively, you will get negative results; if you impress your subconscious constructively, you will get constructive results.

There Is Only One Power

The most important truth you can learn is that there is only one power. This power is omnipresent. Accordingly, it must be within you – your very life. When you use this power constructively and harmoniously and according to its inner nature, men call it God or good. When you use this power within you negatively and destructively, men call it by names like the devil, Satan, evil, hell, misfortune etc. Be honest with yourself and ask yourself this simple question: 'How am I using the power within me?' Right there you will have the answer to your own problem. It is as simple as that.

There Are Many Ways to Pray

If someone asked me how I pray, I would respond by saying that, to me, prayer means the contemplation of the eternal verities or truths of the Infinite from the highest possible standpoint. These truths never change; they are the same yesterday, today and forever.

How a sailor prayed and was rescued

Last year I conducted a seminar-on-the-sea to Alaska. In talking with one of the sailors, he told me that in the last war his ship had been torpedoed and all the men were lost, save himself. He found himself in a raft on the high seas where all he could think of was God. He had no idea of the laws of his mind but in this extreme circumstance he kept saying to himself over and over again, 'God saves me,' and he lapsed off into unconsciousness. When he awoke he found himself on board a British cruiser, the captain of which said to him that he had had an overpowering hunch to change his course. The sailor was espied by a ship's officer on the watch.

This sailor prayed to what he believed was a God up there somewhere –a sort of anthropomorphic being – which might or might not listen to his prayers and entreaty. He had what he called a sort of blind faith and went all the way out on the limb trusting God. Undoubtedly, his simple faith or blind belief impregnated his own subconscious mind, which responded to his belief and saved him.

To look at it from the standpoint of mental and spiritual laws, the wisdom of his subconscious mind knew where the closest ship was and it acted on the mind of the captain, compelling him to change his course and thereby bring about the rescue.

There is no time or space in your subconscious mind; it is co-existent with all wisdom, all power. Actually, all the attributes, qualities and potencies of God are within your subjective depths or whatever other name you care to use. You can call this Inner Wisdom, Universal Mind, the Life-Principle, Subliminal Mind or Super-conscious Mind. Actually, it is nameless. All you need to know is that there is a wisdom and an infinite intelligence within you that far transcends your intellect and ego or your five senses. It is always responsive to your recognition, faith and expectancy. In the sailor's extremity, he placed all his trust in God, believing somehow that he would be rescued. This belief was impregnated in his subconscious, which responded according to his belief.

> *If thou canst believe, all things are possible to him that believeth.* – Mark 9:23

Why the Prayer of Petition Is Generally Wrong

It is wrong for a reason.

> *Before they call, I will answer; and while they are yet speaking, I will hear* – Isaiah 65:24.

No matter what you seek it already is, for all things subsist in the Infinite within you. The way out, the answer, the healing presence, love, peace, harmony, joy, wisdom, power and strength, all these and much more, exist now and are awaiting your call and recognition.

Peace is now. Love is now. Joy is now. Harmony is now. Wealth is now. Guidance is now. Right action is now. The Healing Presence is now, plus the solution to any problem under the sun. The creative ideas of the infinite mind within you are countless and numberless. All you have to do is to claim, feel, know and believe that the answer is yours now. The solution will come.

All things subsist in the Infinite Mind as ideas, images, archetypes or mental patterns in your mind and as you identify with what you seek and claim it boldly, you will get your answer. That is scientific prayer. When you beg and beseech, you are admitting you don't have what you want now. It is this sense of lack that attracts more loss, lack and limitation.

The God you are beseeching has already given you everything. You are here to appropriate and meditate on the reality of your idea or desire. Rejoice and give thanks, knowing that as you contemplate the reality of your desire, idea, plan or purpose, your subconscious will bring it to pass. Be a good receiver. The gifts of God have been given to you from the foundation of time. You must accept your good now. Why wait for it? All things you need are now.

All things exist as ideas in the Infinite and there is a mental pattern behind everything in the universe. Suppose some holocaust destroyed all the engines in the world; engineers could run them off the assembly line by the millions, the reason being that everything you see in the world came out of either the mind of man or the mind of the Infinite. The idea, desire, invention or play in your mind is as real as your hand or heart. Nourish it with faith and confidence and it will be objectified on the screen of space.

Where Is God's Dwelling Place?

God is Spirit. Spirit is omnipresent and within you as well as all in the universe.

> *For ye are the temple of the living God; as God hath said, I will dwell in them.* – II Corinthians 6:16

> *Behold, I stand at the door and knock: if any man hear my voice and open the door, I will come in to him and will sup with him and he with me.* – Revelation 3:20

This quotation points out the intimacy in prayer where you actually conduct a dialogue or commune with your Higher Self. You are not really outside supplicating a distant deity who may or may not answer your prayer. You know your prayer is already answered but you must recognise it, make contact, accept completely and the response will come.

The Supreme Intelligence or Life Principle in your subconscious is always knocking at the door of your heart. For example, if you become ill, the Life Principle will urge you to be well. It is always saying to you, 'Rise up higher; I have need of you.' Open the door to your heart and boldly affirm:

> I know and I believe that the infinite healing presence which created me can heal me. I claim wholeness, vitality and perfection now. Infinite Intelligence in my subconscious is knocking at the door of my heart, reminding me that the answer and way out are within me. My mind is open and receptive to the Infinite Wisdom. I give thanks for the solution that comes clearly into my conscious, reasoning mind.

God is that universal wisdom and power available to all men regardless of creed or colour. God will answer the atheist or agnostic just as well as the saint or the Holy Man; the only prerequisite is belief.

> *If thou canst believe, all things are possible to him that believeth.* – Mark 9:23

Is God a Person or Is God a Principle?

To think of God as an anthropomorphic being or a sort of glorified man with all the whims, eccentricities and peculiarities of man – is neurotic infantilism and absolutely absurd. God is personal to you in this sense: You can at this very moment contemplate love, peace, harmony, joy, beauty, wisdom, power and guidance. As soon as you will begin to express these qualities because you become what you contemplate. You have personalised or individualised the qualities of God. God is boundless love, absolute harmony, absolute joy, boundless wisdom, supreme intelligence and infinite life, which is omnipresent and omnipotent. God is also law, for this is a universe of law and order.

All the elements of personality are within the Infinite Being within you and as you contemplate the qualities of God within you, you will develop a marvellous and wonderful God-like personality. You, at the same time, are operating the law of God or of your own subconscious, because whatever you claim, appropriate or meditate on is impressed into your subconscious mind while your subconscious manifests what is impressed upon it. You could not develop a wonderful personality without using the law, because the law is that your thought and feeling create your destiny – you are what you contemplate.

God is all there is, in all, over all as well as all in all. Stop beating around the bush. Realise that God is the infinite personality and law. These are the two pillars mentioned in the Bible.

> *And he set up the right pillar and called the name thereof Jachin (the one law): and he set up the left pillar and called the name thereof Boaz (infinite personality).*– I Kings 7:21

Many say to me in substance, 'I can't pray to a principle.' They seem to want an old man in the sky to comfort them, forgive them and take care of them like a human father. That attitude is extremely primitive and childish. Remember that the nature of infinite intelligence within you is responsiveness. When you call upon it believingly: it becomes the embodiment of your ideal.

You can't develop a magnetic or wonderful spiritual personality without using the law of your mind. You must establish the mental equivalent of everything you want to be, to do or to have. An emotional welling up or a pious sentimentality toward a distant deity, hoping all the while that you will be transformed, may only lead to neurosis and confusion.

> *Love is the fulfilling of the law* – Romans 13:10

God will become very personal to you as you regularly and systematically fill your soul with love and joy, peace and harmony; and having appropriated these qualities, you will express them. God is love and the best thing you could do is to stop begging, beseeching and praying for that which has already been given you.

Many Use Affirmative Prayer

In this approach, which millions follow in America today, people do not beg God for anything but, instead, recall the great truths which never fail, such as

The Lord is my Shepherd; I shall not want – Psalm 23:1,

which means to them that men shall never want for evidence of the fact that they have chosen the Lordly Power or God, to guide them, watch over them, sustain them and strengthen them, because they know that the word 'shepherd' means their deep conviction of God's love and guidance, which will lead them to green pastures (abundance) and still waters (the quiet mind). That is prayer.

The Prayer of Invocation

When you invoke the blessings, protection and guidance of the Infinite believingly, the answer will come. St. Augustine, when the enemy was knocking at the door of the city of Hippo, of which he was Bishop, found comfort, rest and protection in the following prayer of invocation, which came from his heart:

> Let my soul take refuge from the crowding turmoil of worldly thoughts beneath the shadow of thy wings; let my heart, this sea of restless waves, find peace in thee, O God.

Following this prayer, he went to sleep and found rest for his soul.

POINTS TO REMEMBER...

1. Every person answers their own prayer, whether they are aware of it or not. Whatever a person believes to be true in the conscious mind is accepted in the subconscious, regardless of whether his belief is true or false. For example, if he has

a belief or conviction that he will fail in his examination, his subconscious has no other alternative than to compel him to fail, no matter how hard he may try to succeed objectively.

2. When under hypnosis your conscious mind is suspended in abeyance, your subconscious is open to the suggestions of the operator. No matter how weird or false the suggestion may be, your subconscious will dramatise it as far as possible in order to conform with the nature of the suggestion. Your subconscious is a one-track mind and does not reason, weigh, investigate and differentiate like your conscious mind. Your subconscious reasons deductively only; that is to say, if your conscious mind gives it a false premise, it will with amazing acumen and sagacity dramatise the response to correspond with the nature of the suggestion. Hence, feed your subconscious only with premises that are true, lovely, noble and God-like.
3. God is the creator or infinite intelligence, in your subconscious, which responds to you according to your belief, for the nature of infinite intelligence is responsiveness. Any idea that you emotionalise and feel to be true is impressed in your subconscious and what is impressed (good or bad) is expressed. This is why everyone answers their own prayer. Negative beliefs regarding illness or problems result in the subconscious response according to this belief. in that case and in that way, the prayer is answered. Actually, all prayers are answered and there is no such thing as an unanswered prayer.

And all things, whatsoever ye shall ask in prayer, believing, ye shall receive. – Matthew 21:22

4. The answer to any question is within you before you ask. All that is necessary is for you to recognise that no matter what you seek, the answer is within the infinite presence and power of your subconscious. When you claim the solution expect an answer. According to your faith it will be done. .

The infinite presence and power within your deeper mind, which created the universe and all things, knows all, sees all and has the know-how of accomplishment. To beg and plead is to admit you don't have it. You are, therefore, attesting to lack and limitation. This way you will inevitably attract more misery and loss because whatever you give attention to, your mind magnifies. The idea, desire, mental image, invention, play, book, no matter what is a reality in your mind, is just as real as your hand or heart. Nourish your desire with faith and expectancy.

5. If you have a blind belief in a guardian angel, your subconscious mind will respond with an inner voice or impulse, such as an inner feeling to go in a certain direction, a sort of overpowering hunch, called the inner-silent-knowing of the soul. The angel is the idea that wells up from your deeper mind and solves your problems. Whether the object of your faith is true or false, your subconscious will respond to the conscious mind's belief.
6. If you do not recognise the wisdom, power or intelligence within your subjective depths, it is just the same as if it were not there.

Paul says: Stir up the gift of God, which is in thee

– II Timothy 1:6.

7. A young man with little experience competed for a pilot's position with 2500 applicants who knew more than he did; he pictured himself as a pilot, imagining that he was wearing the insignia and uniform of a pilot. He pictured himself piloting a plane. He kept this vivid imagery up so that his subconscious accepted his mental picture and against tremendous odds he was selected as one of the top men for the ten vacancies. This young man knew the workings of his subconscious mind.
8. For God all are equal. The laws of your mind and the universe

are constant and invariable. It is foolish, childish and absurd to think that, by begging and beseeching a God in the sky, the law of your mind or the universe will be suspended on your behalf. Again, I would like to emphasise that you answer your own prayer. Your subconscious reveals the impress of your thought and responds according to the nature of the impressions made upon it.

9. There is only one power in the universe – not two, three or 100, just one. When you use this power constructively, men call it God; when you use it negatively, ignorantly or destructively, men call it the devil, evil, hell, etc.
10. People pray in many ways. I look upon prayer as the contemplation of the truths of God from the highest standpoint. When you fill your mind with the truths of God, which never change, you neutralise and obliterate all the negative patterns in your subconscious. Whatever you contemplate you become. Anything you consciously claim and feel to be true your subconscious will dramatise and project on the screen of space. That is true prayer.
11. Many men who have no idea how prayer works and who have weird, grotesque and also childish ideas about God, in dire conditions, petition God to save them; and many having a childish belief that some God in the sky will save them, are saved and rescued. The reason for this is that whether the object of your faith is true or false, you will get the same results, as your subconscious doesn't question your belief and reasons deductively only.
12. To beg and beseech a distant deity is to admit that you don't have what you seek now and this attitude attracts more lack and limitation; therefore, you get the opposite of what you want. The Bible says:

What things so ever ye desire, when ye pray, believe that ye receive them and ye shall have them – Mark 11:24

You believe the oak is in the acorn but you must plant the seed; likewise, no matter what your problem, regardless of how difficult it may seem to be, the answer is in the form of a desire. Your desire is the seed, which has its own mathematics, mechanics and manner of expression. Your desire is as real as your hand or your heart.

It is just the same as the idea of a radio is real in your mind. Realise – the infinite intelligence in your subconscious, which is the only creative power, can bring your desire to fulfilment. Believe in the reality of your idea and desire now. Nourish it with faith and confidence. Like a seed, which is watered and fertilised in the ground, it will grow to come above the ground. It will rise in your life as the answered prayer. This is why you can believe you have it now – in your mind it is a reality.

13. You are the temple of the Living God. God is the Living Spirit Almighty within you. Your own mind is where you walk and talk with the only creative power you know. The only immaterial power you are aware of is your thought. Your thought is creative and you know what you are creating now. The life-principle in you is forever knocking at the door of your heart, saying to you, 'Rise, transcend, grow, advance, move forward, open the door of your heart,' and realise there is that within you which can wipe away all tears, heal a sick body, reveal hidden talents and set you on the high road to happiness, freedom and peace of mind.
14. God (Spirit) has all the elements of personality, such as choice, volition, love, peace, harmony, joy, beauty, power, strength, wisdom and intelligence. God is also Law. There can't be one without the other. How could you develop a wonderful personality unless you appropriated, meditated on and ruled into your subconscious only the attributes, qualities and potencies of God? The law is that you become what you claim and feel to be true. In other words, you are what you

contemplate and incorporate into your subconscious. This is done according to the law of your subconscious mind. An emotional swelling of the heart and a pious sentimental attitude to a distant deity leads to confusion, neurosis and disillusionment. Law and personality are one. In order for the Universal Presence and Power to work through the individual, It must first become the individual. You must appropriate in your own thought and feeling the truths of God and then God will be very personal to you. But God is not a person, if by that you mean a sort of glorified man in the sky. Such a concept could be called neurotic infantilism.

15. You can affirm certain great truths. By repetition, faith and expectancy, you will believe and accept them to be true. In that way your affirmative prayer will work. All you are doing is convincing yourself that what you affirm is true and after a while you begin to realise that three and three are six, not seven; then the result follows. St Augustine's Prayer of Invocation, which evoked a response, was:

    Let my soul take refuge from the crowding turmoil of worldly thoughts beneath the shadow of thy wings; let my heart, this sea of restless waves, find peace in thee, O God.

7

HOW TO USE TELEPSYCHICS FOR THE PRAYER THAT NEVER FAILS

Many men and women have said to me repeatedly: 'We have earnestly and sincerely desired certain things, which we have never experienced. We have prayed, longed for, waited and yet failed to get answers.' Then they asked the usual question: 'Why?' The response is that according to your faith your prayers are answered.

What Is Faith?

The faith we speak of in this book does not refer to creeds, dogma, tradition, ritual, ceremonies or any specific religious persuasion. Look upon faith as a mental attitude – a certain way of thinking. Faith is a conscious potentiality whereby you know that any idea you emotionalise and feel to be true is impressed on your subconscious mind and whenever you succeed in impregnating your deeper mind with any idea, plan or purpose, the latter will objectify the impression made on the screen of space. Your subconscious is the creative power within you. Your conscious mind chooses but it does not create. You are, as a matter of fact, the sum total of your choices. Most people do not realise this, while millions reject this truth altogether. Faith, therefore, is a mode of thinking, a manner of believing, a mental acceptance.

A chemist has faith in the laws of chemistry, which are dependable; a farmer has faith in the laws of agriculture; and an engineer has faith in the laws of mathematics. Likewise, man should learn to have faith in the laws of his mind by learning how his conscious and subconscious mind functions and he should understand the interaction of these two phases of his mind.

The prayer of faith and how to use it

The prayer of faith may be looked upon as a mental or spiritual conviction that there is an infinite intelligence in your subconscious mind, which responds to you by the simple process of corresponding with your mental conviction toward the law of your mind. The Bible says:

> *According to your faith be it unto you* – Matthew 9:29
>
> *If thou canst believe, all things are possible to him that believeth* – Mark 9:23

This means that the wisdom and power of your subconscious works through at the level of your belief. To believe is to accept something as true. When you break the word 'believe' down, it means to be alive, to live in the state of being; in other words, be alive to the truths of life, animate the eternal verities, feel the reality of them and you will experience the result of what you incorporate in your subconscious mind.

Why Some Prayers Are Answered and Others Are Not

A man said to me: 'My wife's prayers are always answered; mine are not. Why?' He added that he believed God was withholding good from him for some obscure reason, while favouring his wife because of her religious beliefs. My explanation, however, was somewhat along the following lines: For God all are equal. Any man can learn to use the laws of nature, provided he equips himself with the necessary knowledge.

A murderer or an atheist can learn the laws of electricity and can use this knowledge to wire and light a house. Similarly he can learn the laws of navigation or any other law and apply these laws according to their nature. An atheist can receive an answer from the subconscious as well as can a holy man; the only requirement is belief or complete mental acceptance of the answer.

An astronaut who denies the existence of a Divine Presence can reach Mars, Venus and other planets provided he has sufficient faith and confidence. That is, he believes that whatever he needs to know will be provided by the creative intelligence of his subconscious, because the latter responds to the conscious mind's belief and conviction.

To think that God or Infinite Intelligence, responds to some men and women because of their religious persuasion would be ascribing to God the peculiarities, whimsicalities and inconsistencies of the human mind. God or the Creative Power, existed before any man ever walked the Earth or before any church was ever formed. Men invented the various religious creeds, forms, rituals and dogmas. God is the same yesterday, today and forever. It is silly to think that God withholds from some while giving to others. That would be favouritism, which is unthinkable and absolutely absurd.

As thou hast believed, so be it done unto thee. – Matthew 8:13

This refers to the law of cause and effect, which is cosmic and universal and certainly is no respecter of persons. The cause is your conscious mind's belief and the effect is the response from your subconscious.

He was unconsciously denying what he affirmed

The above-mentioned man was praying for prosperity and affirming: 'God is my instant supply and His wealth is circulating in my life now.' But he admitted that deep down in his heart his belief was in lack and limitation. In other words, his conscious affirmation was denied by his subconscious disbelief.

The reason his wife's prayers were answered is that her faith was much deeper; she really believed what she affirmed. It made sense to her that there is an impersonal presence and power in her subconscious that operates on her habitual thinking and beliefs and that it responds alike to each and all.

How he changed his belief

This man learned a simple truth: that thought becomes a thing in the same way that a seed becomes a plant. His false belief in lack was dissolved in his subconscious mind by a repetition of truth in his conscious mind. He realised that wealth was a thought-image in his mind and that all things come forth from the invisible mind of man or God. This new insight and understanding gave him faith and confidence.

He clearly perceived that a drop of clear water that persistently falls into a bottle of dirty water will eventually show the bottle to be full of clear water. Repetition is the key. This false belief, which this man recognised to be false – was displaced by the continuous repetition of the idea of wealth circulating in his life. Freely, joyously and endlessly.

It was an intellectual statement in the beginning with him, in which his emotion and feeling played no part; but as he continued to repeat the statement, 'Wealth is circulating in my life and there is always a surplus,' with the sincere desire to believe it, the moment came when the last resistance 'let go,' the same as the constant dropping of clear water washed away the last drop of muddy water from the bottle.

When prayer ceases to be true prayer

Recently a woman wrote me, saying that she had to have $6000 by the 15th of the following month; otherwise she would be unable to pay the note due on her mortgage and would lose her home. She added that she was praying very hard to get the $6000 from some source but that she met only with a negative response everywhere.

This woman was anxious, tense, worried and full of fear. I explained to her that her attitude of mind would only attract more loss, lack, limitation and obstacles of all kinds.

> *For the thing which I greatly feared is come upon me.*
> – Job 3:25

The Bible gives the answer to anxiety and fear in a very simple way when it says:

> *In quietness and in confidence shall be your strength.*
> – Isaiah 30:15

Accordingly, at my suggestion, she began to rehearse some of the great truths with which she was familiar but with which she neglected to identify. She began to knowingly affirm the following:

> *But with God all things are possible.* – Matthew 19:26

> *If thou canst believe, all things are possible to him that believeth.* – Mark 9:23

> *He shall call upon me and I will answer him: I will be with him in trouble; I will deliver him and honour him.*
> – Psalm 91:15

> *The Lord is my light and my salvation; whom shall I fear?*
> – Psalm 27:1

Widely regarded as the greatest writer in the English language and the world's pre-eminent dramatist, William Shakespeare, too averred, 'All things be ready if the mind be so.'

She ceased thinking of the needed amount altogether as also the date but she began to reiterate the above great truths, realising that when her mind is at peace, the solution follows. She kept in tune with the Infinite, knowing that God supplies all her needs and is her instant and everlasting supply and support.

I emphasised the simple truth that when her mind was at peace, when she had a Divine indifference, the answer, the solution, was sure to come. Divine indifference means that you know that it is impossible for your prayer to fail, in the same way you are absolutely positive that the sun will rise in the morning. You don't know how the answer will come. You don't really care, because you know whatever happens will be good – very good.

She maintained her peaceful attitude by reminding herself of the great truths that never change. At the end of a week, she met an old school friend in the local drug store. He was a widower and she a widow. He proposed marriage. She accepted, he also took care of the mortgage. She did not lose anything; she gained. Her subconscious magnified and multiplied exceedingly the good she impressed upon it.

Fear and worry attract loss. Faith and confidence in the law of your mind attract all the blessings of life. Whenever the idea comes to you that you must have a certain amount and that it must appear on a certain day, remember that the attitude of mind is usually one of excess tension, anxiety and fear, which produces more loss. Go back to the Source of all blessings. Identify with the Infinite and claim peace, guidance, harmony, right action and abundance. Maintain your contact and the day will break and all the shadows will flee away.

She said she had absolute faith that she would sign the contract

An actress said to me that she had absolute faith that she would get the contract she desired, because she received a phone call from New York to fly there and sign it. When she arrived in New

York, the particular man who was to give her the contract had passed away in his sleep and she returned somewhat disappointed and depressed.

I explained to her that the only thing in which she could have absolute faith was: God is God and that the Laws of the universe are the same yesterday, today and forever. They are dependable, as God and His laws are constant and invariable. Furthermore, I explained to her that she does not control the universe and she has no power over the lives of people. Surely if the man who was to give her the contract was at the point of transition, she had nothing to do with it but that she could always be absolutely certain that God is God – omnipotent, eternal, changeless and timeless.

Telepsychics in Action

She changed her attitude of mind to realise that the infinite intelligence of her subconscious had ways of bringing her desire to pass but that its ways are at times mystical, not easy to find out. She quietly affirmed as follows:

I know that the infinite intelligence within my subconscious has ways of bringing about a business contract in ways not known to my intellect I recognise this transcendental wisdom. I accept a similar contract now or something grander and greater in the wisdom of my deeper mind.

In a few weeks' time she received a much better contract than the one she would have signed in New York City. When something similar to this happens to you, rejoice and be grateful, knowing in your heart that the infinite intelligence within you has something far more wonderful for you. It will come to pass in ways unknown to you. .

Telepsychics teaches you to put confidence in the right place

A brilliant woman who was also a prominent executive in a

business organisation said that she was absolutely sure she would marry a certain man. All the arrangements had been made – the ceremony had been planned, guests invited and the post-nuptial banquet partially paid for; but just minutes before the ceremony, her fiancé dropped dead of a heart attack.

She said, 'Why did God do this to me?' Actually, God was not 'responsible' for the man's demise. The man in question had the capacity to choose and direct his life in any way he wished. Subsequent events showed that he was an alcoholic (which his fiancé did not know) and had been treated for a cardiac condition, having been hospitalised many times. He had hidden all of this from her.

I pointed out to her that, after all, she did not control the man's life nor did she determine when he would go on to the next dimension. Actually, she should rejoice and be exceedingly glad the wisdom of her subconscious mind, which always seeks to protect, heal, restore and guide her, actually prevented her from entering into what would have proved to have been a tragic marriage.

She learned also a simple truth: that you cannot be absolutely certain about anything in this universe except that God is God – that the laws of the universe are constant and invariable. How could anyone be absolutely sure that he will reach San Francisco tomorrow? Maybe fog would intervene and all flights would be cancelled. How could you be absolutely sure your horse would win the race? Maybe the horse might drop dead due to a heart attack. How can you be absolutely sure you will marry that girl? Maybe she will pass on tonight or run off with another man. Are you in control of people and the world?

An old hymn, 'Abide with Me' says:

Change and decay all around I see.
Oh, Thou, Who changeth not, abide with me.

At all times, remember that the wisdom of your subconscious

has ways of bringing about an answer to your prayer that your conscious mind does not know and could not even imagine.

The woman we are writing about never prayed in the right way for a husband. She had met the man in a bar. The romance, along with all his lies and deceit, started from there. In prayer, you should never think of any specific man. You marry character. You do not get what you want in the world but you get what you are – you are what you contemplate.

In order to attract the right spouse, you should build the qualities you admire in a man into your subconscious mind by thinking with interest on the characteristics you esteem and value. I gave her the following prayer and suggested that she use it night and morning:

I know that I am one with God now. In Him I live, move and have my being. God is Life; this Life is the Life of all men and women. We are all sons and daughters of the one Father.

I know and believe there is a man waiting to love and cherish me. I know that I can contribute to his happiness and peace. He loves my ideals while I love his ideals. He does not want to make me over; neither do I want to make him over. We have mutual love, freedom and respect.

There is one mind; I know him now in this mind. I unite now with the qualities and attributes that I admire and want expressed by my husband. I am one with them in my mind. We know and love each other already in the Divine Mind. I see the God in him; he sees the God in me. Having met him within, I must meet him in the without; for this is the law of my own mind.

These words go forth and accomplish wherever they are sent. I know it is now done, finished and accomplished in God. Thank you, Father.

The above words gradually sank into her subconscious mind and the wisdom of her deeper mind attracted to her a wonderful young dentist who harmonised with her in every respect. She learned to place her confidence in the laws of her mind, which never fail. She knew when the content of this prayer reached her subconscious, because she no longer desired to pray for a husband. She had reached a conviction that caused the instant response.

Telepsychics teaches you how to handle all kinds of setbacks

Suppose you have an important appointment with someone in Houston, Dallas or Boston and you are delayed due to fog, sickness etc. You might say that you prayed about the interview – that it would be satisfactory and that Divine order would prevail. Relax; let go; turn to the infinite intelligence of your subconscious and realise that the inner wisdom has better ways of bringing about this interview, contract or whatever it is. Remain poised and calm, knowing that Divine right action prevails. Remember also that your conscious, reasoning mind doesn't know how Divine right action comes to pass.

> *In quietness and in confidence shall be your strength.*
>
> – Isaiah 30:15

Know that God is always God. When you claim and believe that God is in action in your life, then whatever happens will be good – especially good. This really is the prayer that never fails.

POINTS TO REMEMBER

1. Faith is a way of thinking. It is an attitude of mind. You have faith in the laws of mind when you know that whatever is impressed on your subconscious mind will be expressed as experience and events in your life. Any idea you emotionalise and feel to be true, whether good or bad, will be accepted by your subconscious and will come to pass.
2. A farmer has faith in the laws of agriculture. The captain in charge of the ship has faith in the laws of navigation. They are using principles that existed before man walked the earth. Likewise, you can begin to learn the laws of your mind and

transform your whole life. Think good and good follows; think of loss and limitation: misery follows.

3. Your beliefs will determine your conditions and circumstances. This is why Dr Quimby said in 1847, 'Man is belief expressed.' Belief is a thought in your mind. It means to accept something as true. You can also believe a lie but you can't prove it. Believe (be alive) means to be alive to the truths of God. You need to saturate your mind with the eternal verities to transform your whole life into a pattern of harmony, health, peace and abundance.
4. God sees all as equal. He plays no favourites. To think that God responds to some because of their religious beliefs or affirmations of a specific creed is childish sentimentality. God is the universal wisdom and power, available to all men according to their belief and their mental acceptance.
5. Many people unconsciously deny what they affirm. For example, a man may outwardly affirm that God is his source and supply yet have a subconscious belief in poverty. He must change his belief and contemplate God's riches and the law of opulence; then his subconscious will respond to the new conscious belief.
6. When you understand the truth that wealth is a thought-image in your mind, then when you constantly reiterate the truth that God's wealth is circulating in your life, you will supplant the subconscious belief in poverty and results will follow. It is somewhat like pouring clear water into a bottle of muddy water: The moment comes when we have a bottle full of clear water.
7. When faced with the problem of having a certain amount of money at a certain date, forget the amount and the date, as this mental attitude tends to produce anxiety, tension and worry, which attract delays, impediments, difficulties and still more worry. Contemplate some of the great truths of the Psalms and other parts of the Bible, which will bring your mind to

peace. Contemplate that God is your instant and everlasting supply, meeting all your needs now and forevermore. When you have a Divine indifference, your prayer will always be answered in ways you know not of.

8. Change eternal is at the root of all things. God never changes. The only thing you can have absolute faith in is the knowledge that God is God, always the same yesterday, today and forever. If you say you have absolute faith that you will sign a contract with John Jones tomorrow, he may pass on to the next dimension or a hundred and one other things could happen to prevent it. Trust the infinite power within your subconscious to bring it to pass some other way and it will do so.
9. Cease thinking that you control the elements, the life span of others or their destiny. Place your faith and confidence in the indwelling God-Presence, knowing that it is God in action in your life and only Divine right action prevails; then, whatever happens will be good and very good. You can have absolute faith in the goodness and love of God in the land of the living and by accepting this truth, wonders will happen as you pray.
10. When praying for a spouse, you must never think of any specific man or woman. In other words, you must never try to manipulate the mind of the other. You marry character, a state of consciousness. Dwell on the characteristics and qualities you like in a man or woman and then know that the deeper currents of your mind will bring both of you together in Divine order.
11. When you claim and believe it is God in action in your life, then whatever happens, it must be good and very good. This type of prayer never fails.

8

HOW TO APPROACH THE MYSTIC SOURCES OF TELEPSYCHICS

> *For my thoughts are not your thoughts, neither are your ways my ways, saith [said] the Lord (your subconscious). For as the heavens are higher than the earth, so are my ways higher than your ways and my thoughts than your thoughts.* – Isaiah 55:8–9

As I was writing this chapter I received a phone call from a woman in New York who had been reading *Psychic Perception: The Magic of Extrasensory Power.** She had been using the meditation given for developing her inner powers and had been experiencing wonderful results. She said that the night just before she was sound asleep, her long-dead husband appeared to tell her to awaken at once and turn off the gas jet before her son would be asphyxiated. She awoke and the smell of gas was very strong. She awoke her son and opened the windows. Her quick action undoubtedly saved his life and her own.

---

*By Dr Joseph Murphy (Parker Publishing Co., Inc., West Nyack, New York, 1971.)

Every night prior to retiring she had been reciting the 91st Psalm, the great prayer of protection. Her subconscious mind consequently dramatised a picture of her deceased husband, knowing that she would give instantaneous attention to his warning. She would not look upon the inner vision as an idle dream or merely as vagaries of the mind. The ways of the subconscious are indeed difficult to understand.

She insisted that it was her 'dead' husband but nothing in the universe ever dies. The flower that blooms once blooms forever. We are constantly in communication with all beings who ever lived or are living now, because there is one mind common to all individual men. Even though you receive an answer from another person, it still is the wisdom of the subconscious mind giving the answer.

All of us are immersed in the one universal mind. I think our big mistake is to think that we are 'in the body.' Your body is in you as an idea. You will have bodies to infinity. You can't conceive of yourself without a body. Actually, it is impossible. This foreshadows and portrays to you that you will always have a body that oscillates at higher frequencies in the next dimension of life.

The reason why her prayer made her worse

One woman said to me that she had a legal problem about which she prayed but her prayers seemed to make matters even worse. Actually, she was putting all her vexations and anxieties in the centre of her attention. She became more troubled than she had been before she prayed. She learned that whatever she gives attention to her mind magnifies.

Following our conversation she reversed her attitude of mind and affirmed as follows:

> I am not alone. God dwells in me and His wisdom brings about a Divine solution in ways I know not of. I now let go and let the wisdom of the Infinite bring about a solution.

She maintained an affirmative attitude of mind and when fear or wrong thoughts came to her mind, she would immediately affirm: 'There is a Divine solution. It is God in action.'

After a few days her fear thoughts lost all momentum and she had a sense of peace. Her relative, who had been contesting the Will in court and who had been deliberately lying on the stand, dropped the case abruptly and a few days afterwards passed quietly on to the next dimension in her sleep.

Your conscious mind cannot perceive of the way your prayer will be answered, as the workings of your deeper mind transcend the intellect and bring about a solution in their own way.

The answer came to him in a strange way

A real estate broker I knew was interested in making a rather large investment in another state. Every night prior to sleep he prayed for divine guidance and right action in all his undertakings. Following one of his visits to the property he was contemplating buying, he had a very vivid dream. The hexagram 33 Retreat of the *Secrets of the I Ching* appeared, which said: 'This is not the time to advance.'

He followed the advice. Subsequent events proved the correctness of his decision, as members of the underworld were involved in the transaction. The reason his subconscious mind presented him with the hexagram 'Retreat' undoubtedly was due to the fact that he had been studying the Secrets of the *I Ching*, which is a book I wrote on the Biblical and psychological meanings of the 64 hexagrams of the *I Ching* or *Book of Changes*, translated by Wilhelm Baynes, with a foreword by the late Carl Jung. All I have done is to give the meanings of the hexagrams in modern, everyday language. Apparently, the subconscious of this real estate broker decided to answer him in a way that he would immediately recognise and obey.

The strange way her prayer was answered

A few Sundays ago, after one of my lectures at the Wilshire Ebell

Theatre, Los Angeles, where I have been lecturing for over twenty-two years, a young lady told me an interesting story. Studying psychology and comparative religions at the local university, she said that she had been praying for guidance as to whether she should go into the ministry to teach mental and spiritual laws on a non-denominational level. She said that a most interesting dream had presented itself to her: that I – appeared to her in her dream – had pointed to Number 30 Hexagram in *Secrets of the I Ching*, which is called Li/The Clinging, Fire.

She read clearly from the book in her sleep the following, which appears under 'The Image' in that hexagram: *And the Light of Israel shall be for a fire...* – Isaiah 10:17. Fire in the Bible and in I Ching means illumination or the Supreme Intelligence of your subconscious mind, revealing to you everything you need to know to enable you to direct that light on others.

On awakening she looked up the hexagram and the words she saw in her dream coincided exactly with what she read under 'The Image' in *Secrets of the I Ching.** She remarked, 'The answer is right and that is what I am going to do.' She understood that her subconscious often times speaks in symbols, as water can be a symbol of the subconscious or fire can mean Infinite Intelligence or Passion.

My appearance symbolised the truth to her in the dream. She is now very happy in her new studies. Being a student of the *I Ching*, her entire dream was very meaningful to her and it satisfied her in every way.

He makes a habit of prayer

While discussing the subject of prayer with a Chinese student in Hawaii, he said that his technique of prayer is based on a spiritual companionship as he prays. He converses frequently with his

---

*See *Secrets of the I Ching* by Dr Joseph Murphy (Parker Publishing Company, Inc., West Nyack, New York, 1970.)

Higher Self; he has what he terms frequent colloquies or short discourses between his conscious mind and the God Presence within. His approach is somewhat like this as he addresses his Higher Self:

Father, Thou art all wise. Reveal to me the answer, guide me in my studies, tell me what to do, reveal my talents to me and give me wisdom and an understanding heart.

There are times, he claims, when he has a complete prevision of all the questions he is about to be asked at a forthcoming examination and he has no problem with his studies. Once he heard an inner voice telling him to study the *I Ching* or *Book of Changes*, which he did. He said it became a great aid in self-discovery.

A very wealthy woman on one of the islands asked him to read the *I Ching* for her. She wanted to know: 'Would it be a wise course for me to have the major operation that has been suggested?' She received Hexagram 30, The Clinging/Fire. The judgement said: 'Care of the cow brings good fortune.'

He explained to her the meaning of the cow, in Chinese symbolism. Cows are gentle creatures, which require looking after and it means good fortune can be gained from looking after the cow (subconscious mind). He said that she was full of resentment, suppressed rage and hostility. She made out a list of all those whom she resented and hated and began to pour out blessings, love and goodwill on them. She also forgave herself for harbouring destructive thoughts and emotions. By filling her subconscious mind (taking care of the cow) with life-giving patterns, she had a remarkable healing and as a reward gave him a present of $5000 to further his studies. This Chinese student discovered that the glory of the Infinite within him is in spiritual habitual companionship.

To build character, practice is a must. It is necessary to contemplate the eternal truths. As we do, we become what we contemplate in thought, word, deed in all phases of our lives.

Prayer Is Your Heart's Desire Also

When sick, you desire health; when poor, you desire wealth; if hungry, you desire food; and if thirsty, you desire water to quench your thirst. If lost in the woods, you desire to know the way home. You desire to express yourself as well as find your true place in life. Your desire is life's urge within you, reminding you of a void in your life that you should fill. If you are an inventor, you desire to have your invention patented and put on the market. You desire to be loved, wanted, needed and useful to humanity.

Desire is the cause of all feeling and action. It is the Life Principle seeking to express Itself at higher levels through you.

Desire is Life seeking to manifest Itself in some form, which as yet exists only as thought-image in your mind. Desire is the force behind all things; it is the moving principle of the universe.

Remember, your desire has fulfilment for its correlation. Desire and fulfilment could be considered somewhat similar to the law of cause and effect. The Bible says: *Blessed are they that hunger and thirst after righteousness, for they shall be filled* – Matthew 5:6. Blessed are all those who hunger and thirst to do right, think right, act right, be right and live right according to the golden rule and the law of love.

She decided to be a gangway and channel for God

Some months ago I received a letter from an English actress who had been out of work for several months and all doors seemed to be closed to her. I suggested to her that she establish the right relationship with the Infinite Presence within her and let the Divine Presence flow through her, thereby letting the wisdom and power direct her in all ways.

She talked to her Higher Self and affirmed:

> I surrender to the Infinite Intelligence within me and I know God flows through me as harmony, true expression,

beauty, right action and Divine activity. I know that all that is required of me is to become an open channel and let His life, love, harmony and creative ideas flow through me.

Following this new mental attitude, she was offered an opportunity to participate in a movie in France and another in Italy. She is now active in TV in London. All doors opened up for her. She had been blocking her good by fear, worry and excess tension, somewhat similar to putting your foot on the hose when you are watering the garden. Prayer is the listening ear, i.e., we must hear the truth to realise that God, who gave us a certain talent, will also reveal the perfect plan for it to unfold. We must have an open and receptive heart and let the influx of Divine Life flow through us, realising that it is as easy for God to become harmony, health, peace, abundance, true expression and love in our experience as it is to become a blade of grass or a crystal of snow.

How prayer healed her emotional spasm

As I was writing this chapter, a woman phoned me from the office of her cardiologist, stating that her heart specialist said that her heart was normal and that he believed her occasional spasms were purely emotional. She seemed to be unreasonably obsessed with the idea that someone was practicing black magic against her.

She visited me later at my request and I explained to her that she was giving power to someone else and that the only Power was the Living Spirit within her, that It is one and indivisible and that there is nothing to oppose omnipotence and omniscience and further that it was her own fear thoughts that were hurting her.

I suggested that she artfully and subtly instil in her mind the contents of the 27th Psalm until she let go of the false ideas. In about a week's time she had broken the spasmodic grip. She practiced the great law of substitution by repeating the great truths of the Psalm over and over again until her mind gripped the truth, setting her free.

A simple illustration of how to do this is as follows: Take a bottle of muddy water and let drop by drop of clear water fall into the mouth of the bottle. The moment always comes when you will have a bottle of clear water.

POINTS TO REMEMBER

1. Your subconscious seeks to protect you at all times but you must listen to its inner promptings, monitions and urges. Oft-times the answer to a particular problem will come to you in a very vivid dream, which proves very meaningful to you. A woman said that her dead husband warned her in a dream that the gas jet was on. This was a dramatisation of her subconscious mind in response to her constant nightly prayer of protection using the 91st Psalm.
2. When you pray, do not put all your anxieties and troubles at the centre of your attention. Focus on the solution, knowing that the wisdom of your subconscious will reveal the answer or solution in ways you know not of. Maintain an affirmative attitude of mind. When fear comes, supplant the fear with faith in God and all things good.
3. It is a good practice to pray regularly for divine guidance and right action in all your undertakings. If you are a student of the Bible or the Secrets of the *I Ching* you will find that often times your subconscious may answer with a phrase from Proverbs or give you a specific hexagram that reveals the perfect answer.
4. One student received in a dream the 30th Hexagram of Secrets of the I Ching as an answer to her question: Should she study for the ministry? The instruction connected with the hexagram said: *And the light of Israel shall be for a fire.*– Isaiah 10:17. Fire in the Bible and in *I Ching* means light and illumination, enabling her to direct that light or inspiration

on others. She is now studying mental and spiritual laws and is very happy.

5. A Chinese student has what he terms frequent dialogues with his Higher Self. His approach is simple: 'Father, Thou art all-wise. Reveal to me the answer, guide me in my studies and tell me what to do.' Many times he has a mental preview in his sleep of all questions to be asked in his examinations. He receives inspiration and insight into the symbolic meaning of the *I Ching*, which has netted him considerable money.
6. Prayer is the soul's sincere desire; desire is the cause of all feeling and action. It is the Life-Principle seeking to express Itself at higher levels through you. Claim that the Life-Principle within you that gave you the desire reveals the perfect plan for its manifestation in Divine order and your subconscious will reveal the perfect plan for its fulfilment.
7. When out of work, surrender to the God-Presence within you and decide to become an open and receptive channel for the flow of the Infinite through you. Say to yourself, 'God flows through me as harmony, beauty, love, peace, right action, true expression and abundance. I know it is as easy for God to become all these things in my life as it is to become a blade of grass or a crystal of snow.' As you make a habit of this, all doors will open up to you. Take your foot off the hose and let the water flow through.
8. If you had a bottle of muddy water and you let drop by drop of clear water enter the mouth of the bottle, the moment would come when you would have clear water. Likewise, when you have an emotional spasm of fear, you can instil the great truths of the 27th Psalm to fill your mind with these wonderful truths. The thoughts of fear will be neutralised – actually destroyed to ensure your peace of mind. This is the great law of substitution.

9

HOW TO USE TELEPSYCHICS AS THE FOURTH-DIMENSIONAL ANSWER TO PRAYER

Down through the ages, man has been fascinated and mystified by his dreams. In ancient times men believed them to be messages from the gods and voyages of the soul to distant lands. The fourth dimension of life is that place to which you travel every night when you go to sleep.

During the 19th Century, many scholars maintained that dreams were merely the fulfilment of suppressed desires, wish fulfilment, dramatisation of sex suppression and other complexes. The late professors Carl Jung and Sigmund Freud believed that all dreams had an inner meaning and were important as dramatisations of inner wishes, desires and frustrations.

However, I have found in my discussions, correspondence and interviews with people of various religions and cultural backgrounds that many of these people dream literally at times as also receive answers to their most acute problems in dreams.

How her dream found a lost diamond

Recently I talked with a woman who said, 'You can imagine how I felt when, upon taking off my gloves at the doctor's office, I found my five-carat diamond ring missing.' Then she added that she had looked frantically everywhere – along the pavement, which she had traversed, in her car, at home and in the garden. It seemed to her as if she were looking for a needle in a haystack.

I suggested to her that she follow a very simple but very old and tested technique: to imagine she was wearing the ring and to feel the solidity, tangibility and naturalness of it. In her imagination she was to take off the ring at night and place it in her jewellery box as she was accustomed to doing prior to retiring every night. All this was to be an imaginary act. While her head was on the pillow, she was to lull herself to sleep with her favourite prayer, 'Thank you, Father,' which meant to her that she was grateful for the return of her ring, knowing that there is nothing lost in the mind of the Infinite.

On the third night, while sound asleep, she saw her ring clearly in the maid's room, wrapped in a piece of paper and located in an old shoe belonging to the maid. She awoke suddenly, went to the bedroom of her maid. The diamond was exactly in the place pictured in her dream. The maid professed to know nothing about it and couldn't imagine how it had managed to reach her shoe. Later on during the day, she confessed to having taken it as well as 50 rare coins worth considerable money.

Here, again, we have evidence of the multiplying power of the subconscious. It gave her the answer plus more than she had asked.

How a child transformed her life

A schoolteacher who had been married to an atheist for several years. Though she agreed with many of his ideas, she found herself in a state of acute depression. She had been taking tranquilisers prescribed for her by her psychiatrist. Brought up in a convent, she had been deeply religious. However, when she had married, her husband ridiculed all religious beliefs as well as further affirmed that all of us were merely a confluence of atoms, that our brains secreted thought etc. She gave lip service to his beliefs in order to keep peace but did not really believe them in her heart. When the effects of the drugs wore off, she found that she had to keep on taking them. Moreover, they caused many side effects when she realised that the trouble was in her mind.

She said that one morning she turned the dial on the radio to KIEV to hear me talking on minds devoid of spiritual understanding and how all sorts of debris, false knowledge and various isms enter in bringing about mental and emotional sickness. She kept listening every morning for about two weeks. Then, during the third week, every night for seven nights she had a very vivid dream in which a little boy with a halo around his head appeared to her and beckoned her to come to him. As she went to meet him and embrace him, he ran away – in her dream she could not catch him. This was repeated every night. On the seventh night he said to her, 'When you catch me you will be healed,' and he disappeared.

I explained to her that the late Carl Jung discovered in his research that in the collective unconscious of the race, there are archetypal images that are common to all people everywhere. His research disclosed that people living in different times and countries have dreamed of the 'luminous child,' the 'sage or wise man,' madonnas, the mother figure, circles, crosses, serpents, mandalas (squares within a circle), the white rose as well as many other symbols.

The luminous child with a halo around his head was an archetypal image luring her to go back to God. The Divine Presence, the Indwelling Power or Spiritual Idea is mentioned in the Bible as a child. The conscious awareness of this Power within you as also your decision to contact and make use of it, is the birth of the child.

Intuitively, she knew that the appearance of the child with the nimbus (symbol of light or illumination) meant that she was to return to communion with the God-Self within her, which is exactly what she did. When the child appeared again she was able to embrace the child.

The first book she studied was *The Power of Your Subconscious Mind** the study and application of which has changed her whole life. She dissolved the marriage, which in reality was no marriage at all but a farce and a masquerade.

How she found the answer to loneliness

A widow, deeply despondent and as she said, frantic with loneliness because her husband and two children were killed in a crash, found the answer to her loneliness by meditating on the truths of the 23rd Psalm two or three times a day.

One night she heard an inner voice; she does not remember whether she was asleep or awake. She distinctly heard the voice saying to her, 'Supply the need in other's lives.' As she woke up with a start – to snap out of her despondency and gloom – she said to herself, I am a nurse., That is what I am going to do.

The next day she visited many of the men at the Veteran's Hospital. She wrote letters for some, gave comforting words to many and read the Psalms to others. This continued for a week, she became full of love and compassion. All the patients welcomed her with delight. She went back to nursing full time and now gives a transfusion of faith and confidence to all those to whom she ministers. She is now truly filling a need. The voice she heard was the voice of intuition: the inner promptings of the subconscious often times manifest in the form of a voice, which no one else hears but the individual himself.

Thousands of years ago, the Upanishads (a collection of mystical philosophic treatises) taught that 'man in his dream

---

*By Dr Joseph Murphy (Prentice-Hall, Inc., Englewood Cliffs, NJ, 1963.)

becomes a creator.' Robert Louis Stevenson, contemplating the dual nature of man, which perplexed him, was shown in a dream emanating from his subconscious the plot which he called *Dr Jekyll and Mr Hyde*.

Similarly, Elias Howe had great difficulty in perfecting the sewing machine. Yet while meditating on the solution, his subconscious responded in a dream, showing him exactly where to place the eye of the needle.

His invisible partner

An old friend of mine, who is an extraordinarily successful man and who often times makes purchases of $500,000+ worth of stocks and bonds, one time said to me, 'You know, Murphy, $500,000 is only a drop in the bucket to what I usually invest.' This man told me that his entire life is governed by an invisible guide. He hears an inner voice that tells him to go ahead with certain investments and says 'No' to others. His constant prayer since he was a boy has been the following: *'I will fear no evil: for thou art with me* – Psalm 23:4. God is my invisible partner and guide. I hear the inner voice which says clearly to me, 'Yes, Yes and No, No.'

Obviously, he has so conditioned his subconscious mind that he hears the inner prompting and warnings as an inner voice, which no one but he can hear. This is clair audience or hearing clearly the ideas of his deeper mind.

How an alcoholic found inner peace and freedom

Some months ago I interviewed an alcoholic, whose wife and sons had died of cancer. He was deeply depressed and melancholic. I explained to him that his sincere desire to give up alcohol was the first step in healing, to which he agreed. The next step was to realise that there is a subjective power within him, which would take away all craving and would compel him to assert his freedom from the habit.

I suggested that he practice a simple technique several times daily, which consisted of imagining that I was congratulating him on his peace of mind and sobriety. He continued to do this for about two weeks, three times daily for about five minutes. One night his wife and two sons appeared to him while he was asleep and said to him, 'Dad, we want you to live. We love you. We are happy and leading a new life. Don't mourn for us.'

This dream had a most profound effect on him and he had an instantaneous healing. He said to me, 'I am free! I have a peace and serenity of mind which I never knew before. I am grateful.'

The Bible says: *Acquaint now thyself with him and be at peace* –Job 22:21. This man had acquainted himself with the power of his thought and imagination. His subconscious responded in a way that brought about instant freedom and peace of mind.

How he found a way out of the wilderness in Vietnam

Recently I talked with a young sergeant. He, together with others, had had to bail out of a plane that had caught on fire and he found himself in the jungle, hopelessly lost. He could find no trace of his comrades. Then he said to himself the only words he knew of the 91st Psalm, called the great Psalm of protection:

> *I will say of the Lord, He is my refuge and my fortress: my God; in Him will I trust.* – Psalm 9:2

He remarked that as he repeated this verse of the Psalm, all fear vanished, then a very strange thing occurred: His brother, who had been killed in action a year before, suddenly appeared to him in full uniform and said, 'Follow me.' He led him to the side of a hill and then said, 'Stay here until morning and you will be safe.' Then he vanished. The next morning at daybreak a patrol found him and he was flown back to camp.

This man overcame his fear and his subconscious responded through the phantasm of his brother, knowing that he would instantly obey and follow his brother. His subconscious also knew where the patrol was and knew he would be cared for.

The ways of the subconscious are beyond our understanding. Remember, your subconscious mind responds in its own way to your prayer of faith.

According to your faith be it unto you. – Matthew 9:29

The explanation that saved the would-be suicide

A depressed young mother who had lost two sons in Vietnam asked me why she should not commit suicide. My explanation was rather simple: 'The problem is in the mind. You are a mental and spiritual being. You are not just your body. Your body is an idea in your mind. You will have bodies to infinity. You don't solve a problem by leaving Los Angeles and running off to Boston. You carry your mind wherever you go. Jumping off a bridge solves nothing. You meet the problem in your mind and solve it there. You are greater than any problem.'

I explained to her that anyone can leave their present body and travel thousands of miles; moreover, they have visual, auditory and tactile capacities outside their body. They can see and be seen; they can enter closed doors, observe everything around them. At the same time, they can see their own bodies on a couch in their home. They have put on a fourth-dimensional body, sometimes called the astral body or subtle body.

I elaborated on the fact that scientists have written about peoples' excursions outside their own body. I described the experiments and research of the late scholar Dr Hornell Hart, former associate of Dr J B Rhine at Duke University, who had investigated numerous cases of peoples' experiences outside the body.

She began to realise intuitively and intellectually that she would meet the same problems outside the body that she now had, because the other astral body, though much more mysterious would not solve any problems. She would remain frustrated and perplexed in her new body, which would conform to her negative thoughts and imagery.

Her suicidal complex was caused by an intense desire for freedom and peace of mind. What she really wanted was greater expression of life, for there is no real extinction of life. Her desire was to overcome the obstacle or difficulty of acute mental depression and melancholia.

I pointed out to her that her boys were functioning in another dimension of mind. Surely they were entitled to her thoughts of love, peace, joy and goodwill. They were not entitled to her radiation of gloom, sorrow and grief. Protracted grief is always morbid selfishness. Love always frees and rejoices in the happiness, peace and welfare of the other.

She decided to go back to work immediately and to surrender her sons to the God Presence.

Whenever she thought of them she immediately affirmed: 'I know where you are God is and His Love fills your soul. God be with you.'

As she practiced this spiritual therapy there was a recrudescence of the Spirit in her life and her vitality and peace of mind were restored.

> *He feedeth among the lilies (truths of God). Until the day break and the shadows flee away*
>
> – Song of Solomon 2:16, 17

POINTS TO REMEMBER

1. The fourth-dimension is that place where you go every night when you drop off to sleep. Many answers to the most perplexing problems are given to you in dreams and symbols. Many people dream literally and find that their dreams come true.
2. A woman lost a valuable diamond ring and failed to find it

anywhere. She began to wear the ring in her imagination, felt the tangibility and naturalness of it and prior to sleep every night said: 'Thank you, Father,' which meant to her that she had already received the ring. After a few nights, while asleep, she saw clairvoyantly where the ring was and discovered it. She saw it covered up in one of her maid's old shoes.

3. A religious woman married to an atheist was frustrated and suffered from suppressed anger toward her husband because he ridiculed all religious beliefs. Her subconscious came to her aid in a dream, showing her the 'luminous child,' a symbol of the awareness of the Presence of God within her. She knew intuitively what it meant and returned to inner communion in thought and feeling with the Divine Presence within her, subsequently receiving a complete healing. She dissolved the marriage, which actually was no marriage but a farce, a sham and a masquerade.
4. A woman overcame loneliness by meditating on the 23rd Psalm. Her subconscious spoke to her in the form of an inner voice, which said: 'Supply a need in others' lives.' Being a nurse, she went back to work and gave a wonderful transfusion of faith, love and confidence to all her patients. All gloom and despondency disappeared. She felt needed, wanted, loved and appreciated. *And thine ears shall hear a word behind thee, saying, This is the way, walk ye in it* – Isaiah 30:21.
5. It was written in the Upanishads thousands of years ago, 'Man in his dream becomes a creator.' Robert Louis Stevenson, while contemplating the dual nature of man, received an answer, a plot of a book, in a dream and called it *Dr Jekyll and Mr Hyde*, which was translated into all known languages.
6. A multimillionaire, who made huge investments from time to time, told me that his entire life is governed by an invisible guide. He hears an inner voice which says 'Yes' to certain investments and 'No' to others. For years he has conditioned his subconscious to respond in this manner. His constant

prayer is 'God (Infinite Intelligence) is my invisible partner and guide and I hear the inner voice, which says clearly to me, 'Yes, Yes' and 'No, No.'

Let your communication be, Yea, yea; Nay, nay
– Matthew 5:37.

7. An alcoholic who had a sincere desire to give up the habit became healed, because he had come to a clear-cut decision. His subconscious reacted according to his definite decision. He used the simple technique of imagining that I was congratulating him on his freedom, peace of mind and sobriety. He immobilised his attention and relaxed. In that relaxed atmosphere, he knew his mental picture, which he emotionalised and felt as true would be impressed on his subconscious and come to pass. His subconscious responded in a rather dramatic and unique way: His deceased wife and two sons appeared to him in a dream and said to him, 'Dad, we want you to live. We are happy where we are.' This fourth-dimensional answer had a profound effect upon him – he experienced instantaneous healing.
8. A sergeant lost in the jungles of Vietnam prayed, using a single verse of the 91st Psalm: *I will say of the Lord, He is my refuge and my fortress: my God; in him will I trust*– Psalm 91:2.
9. The response from his subconscious was unique. His deceased brother appeared to him in uniform and directed him to a place of safety, informing him he would be safe there. A patrol found him the next morning and he was flown back to the camp. The ways of the subconscious are indeed past finding out.
10. A depressed mother who had lost two sons in Vietnam had a suicidal complex, feeling that jumping off a bridge would solve her mental depression. She learned that she has bodies to infinity, that she is not just living in a body but that the

body is an idea or vehicle of expression for her mind and spirit. The problem was in her mind and the suicidal complex was a desire for freedom, not for extinction of life, which could not take place anyway. She quickly grasped the idea that she had to meet the problem in her mind and solve it there, since wherever you go, you carry your mind with you. She released her sons to God and prayed for them regularly by radiating love, peace, harmony, freedom and joy to them and whenever she thought of them, a silent benediction went forth from her: 'God loves you and cares for you.' Her vitality and peace of mind were restored.

Acquaint now thyself with him and be at peace – Job 22:21

10

HOW TELEPSYCHICS RELEASES THE HIGHER POWERS OF YOUR MIND

While writing this chapter, I had a most interesting conversation with a former colonel in the Air Force. He told me that a few years ago he had read an account by the late Dr E R Rawson, which told of how one of his women students had seen in a dream the location of a plane and two men in it. In her dream the plane was on fire and the two men burned to death. She and another woman went to the location and prayed. The plane appeared – was on fire but the men were not touched by the fire.

This account, he said, made a tremendous impression on him. He realised there were higher powers of his mind, which could save him in the midst of a fire or any kind of disaster.

Tuning-in with the higher self saved his life

While serving in Vietnam, the colonel's plane was fired at and exploded in mid-air. In the midst of the fire he bailed out. yet not a hair on his head was singed. He told me he knew that when his plane was on fire, he could not be burned. He demonstrated to himself that at higher dimensions of mind men can't be burned – they become impervious to all harm. Undoubtedly, he had built up this immunity by dwelling on the article he had read about the two women who prayed and saved the two men from the burning plane.

Telepsychics or communicating with the infinite powers of your subconscious mind, is what the Bible means when it says: *If God* (Infinite Power) *be for us, who can be against us?* – Romans 8:31.

How Hindus walk on fire without being burned

Jack Kelley wrote in the newspaper *Enquirer,* from which I quote in part:

> The amazing feats of Hindu fakirs – who seem to defy nature by walking barefoot on burning coals – have baffled men for centuries....At the annual festival of Thaipsam in Singapore, where hundreds walk the fiery coals, Physician Dr Narasionhala Ramaswami explained to the *Enquirer* he has examined fire-walkers for 18 years and not once seen anyone burned or injured. 'The reasons are partly mystic and partly scientific,' he said. 'The mystic part is embraced in belief. It is the power of the mind. Because they tell themselves so hard that they are not going to feel pain, they do not feel pain in a trance-like state of mind.'
>
> Gopala Krishnan, a nineteen-year-old Singapore resident, told the *Enquirer*: 'Beforehand we have to fast. We sleep in the temple and have no contact with our families. All the time we pray. We pray so hard we bring ourselves to a state of trance. Our faith is so strong it guards against any kind of pain, injury or ailment.'

It is said that thought rules the world. Ralph Waldo Emerson said, 'Thought is the property of those only who can entertain it.' Learn to have a healthy, wholesome regard for your thoughts. Your health, happiness, security and protection are largely determined by your awareness of the power of thought.

Thoughts are things and thoughts execute themselves. Your thought is a mental vibration and a definite power; your action is but the outer and worldly manifestation and expression of your individual thought. If your thoughts are wise, your actions will be wise. William Shakespeare said in his play, *Hamlet* 'Our thoughts are ours, their ends none of our own.'

Whatever you think and feel as true, your subconscious will bring to pass. Your thought and feeling create your destiny. Feeling – insofar as your thought is concerned – means interest. This is the meaning of the Biblical phrase: *For as he thinketh in his heart, so is he.* – Proverbs 23:7.

When you are keenly interested in your profession, work or a special assignment, you will be successful because you have your heart in it. You are thinking in depth or feeling the reality of your thought, which is 'thinking in the heart'.

How a detective tapped his subconscious mind

I had a most interesting talk with a detective on the cruise-ship Princess Carla, on which I conducted a seminar on Higher Aspects of Living. He told me that he had been assigned to the Narcotics Squad in an Eastern city. He suspected three men of smuggling large amounts of cocaine and heroin but he and his partners could find no evidence and the case baffled them.

One night he was thinking of the solution and he asked for guidance to be shown the place where they stored the narcotics. He lulled himself to sleep with these words: 'My subconscious gives me the evidence.' He focused all his attention on the word 'evidence,' lulling himself to sleep with the one word, 'evidence, evidence, evidence.' That night he had a very vivid dream in which he saw the three men in a garage. He saw the name, the address and the location of the narcotics.

He got up immediately, arranged for a warrant, called his partners and they raided the place, finding the cocaine and heroin in exactly the place where he saw it in his dream. The value of the seizure was about $3 million.

This detective succeeded in impregnating his subconscious mind with the idea of *evidence.* As the mind reasons deductively only, it gave him a perfect answer. Within your subconscious is infinite intelligence and boundless wisdom. Only it knows the answer.

This detective said that his super conscious watches over him. Often he hears an inner voice telling him where to go and where not to go (clairaudience: the capacity to hear the inner promptings of his deeper mind). The word *superconscious* is simply the I AM or the Presence of God, which is in your subconscious. That is to say, all the powers, qualities and aspects of God are within your subconscious depths. Therefore, when you read the term 'subconscious mind' in this book, it is all-inclusive and means not only the law of God but also all the qualities and powers of God.

This simplifies matters and you don't get confused by a lot of words, such as conscious mind, subjective mind, subliminal mind, super conscious mind, collective unconscious, universal mind, etc.

Many People Are Clairaudient

Socrates, one of the wisest of men of all time, was guided throughout his life on this plane of existence by an inner voice – in which he had implicit belief. 'Do not say that Socrates is buried,' he told his followers. 'Say that you buried my body.' Socrates understood that man was a mental and spiritual being. that a person's soul (Spirit) was immortal – that all they had ever learned was imperishable.

Today we would say that Socrates was clairaudient, as he so often referred to a warning voice in his ear. This undoubtedly was an inner monition from his subconscious mind which prompted him regularly and systematically to do and say the right thing.

A young Japanese student told me that he had been scheduled to go on a plane that was later hijacked in Los Angeles but that he clearly heard an inner voice which said, 'Don't go.' He obeyed it and saved himself from shock, delay and a painful experience.

How telepsychics overcame her anxiety neurosis

Recently, I interviewed a woman who said that her doctor had informed her that she was suffering from 'anxiety neurosis,' which means, in everyday language, chronic worry. I suggested to her that by communicating regularly with her Higher-Self, which is the Living Spirit Almighty or God and which is in the depths of her own subconscious mind, she would get results.

I explained to her that telepsychics is simply the process of contacting all the powers of God within her and that the minute she tuned in with her thought, the powers of God would become active and potent in her life.

The technique she used to overcome her anxiety neurosis was as follows: She began to communicate with her Higher-Self three or four times a day, knowing that inevitably there would be a response. She affirmed the following truths feelingly, meaningfully and knowingly:

> *But there is a spirit in man: and the inspiration of the Almighty giveth them understanding* – Job 32:8. This Almighty Power is within me and I am now surrounded by the sacred circle of God's eternal love. God's river of peace flows through me. God's love fills my soul. My mind is full of peace, poise, balance and equilibrium. I am Divinely guided in all ways. My faith and confidence is in God and all things good. I live with the joyous expectancy of the

best. Whenever fear or worry thoughts enter my mind, I will immediately affirm, 'I exalt God in the midst of me' *for God hath not given us the spirit of fear but of power and of love and a sound mind* – Timothy 1:7.

She identified herself mentally and emotionally with these truths and the secret of her prayer process was that when worry thoughts came to her, she immediately supplanted them with thoughts of God, such as, 'I exalt God in the midst of me.' As she made a habit of this, gradually the thoughts of fear and worry lost all momentum. She was at peace. She has conquered her worries by partaking of the truths of God, which are always the same yesterday, today and forever.

How her faith in god saved her husband's life

On a recent trip to Mexico City, I met an old friend who specialises in acupuncture and who gets what he terms 'miraculous results' with his patients. While I was waiting for him at the hotel, a woman introduced herself, saying, 'Oh! I recognise you. Your picture is in the *Secrets of the I Ching*, which I use all the time. It is a masterpiece.' She then unfolded a remarkable experience with precognition (seeing an event before it happens).

For two consecutive nights in a dream she saw a man aim a rifle at her husband and shoot him dead. She looked upon this at first as a sort of nightmare and awoke horror-stricken. She consulted the *Secrets of the I Ching* and asked what she should do. She received the answer in Hexagram 24, which said:

In returning and rest shall ye be saved; in quietness and in confidence shall be your strength – Isaiah 30:15. *If thou return to the Almighty, thou shall be built up* – Job 22:23. This means, as you align yourself with the Infinite Presence within you, this Power becomes active and potent in your life. In this inner communion with the Divine, you feel the strength, guidance and love of His Presence.

This was the answer she received from the Secrets of the *I Ching*, which is an age-old Chinese method of activating the spiritual agencies of your subconscious mind. She fixed her mind on some of the great truths of the Bible, knowing that only in that way could she save her husband's life.

Before they call, I will answer; and while they are yet speaking, I will hear. – Isaiah 65:24

Thy faith hath made thee whole. – Matthew 9:22

A merry heart maketh a cheerful countenance… – Proverbs 15:13

I am the Lord that healeth [heals] thee. – Exodus 15:26

What things soever ye desire, when ye pray, believe that ye receive them and ye shall have them. – Mark 11:24

She anchored her mind on these passages and also on the 91st Psalm, knowing that God's love watched over her husband. As she saturated her mind with these Biblical truths, she felt a deep, abiding sense of peace and tranquillity. She felt the whole armour of God surround her husband.

A few days later he came home and told her that a man fired three shots at him, all of which missed him; another aimed a pistol at him and tried to fire but each time it failed to go off. It was a miraculous escape. Doubtless, wife's prompt prayer had protected him from certain death. The plan to kill him was already in the subconscious mind and she, being in tune telepathically with her husband, picked it up. By changing the picture in her mind, she could realise through the presence of God where her husband was, to enable to save his life.

Thy faith hath made thee whole – Matthew 9:22

POINTS TO REMEMBER

1. When you enter into a higher level of mind, you are rendered impervious to all harm. It is a very high state of consciousness where you feel aligned with the Infinite, which is all-powerful and all-wise.
2. You build up an immunity to disaster by constantly dwelling on God's love, which surrounds you, enfolds you and enwraps you. You become what you contemplate.
3. There are various rituals in India where some people walk on red hot coals without experiencing any ill effects. Their minds are conditioned over a long period of time. They believe they are protected by their intense faith. They have a subconscious conviction that no harm will come to them. Their blind faith is accepted by their subconscious and in a trance like state – no pains follow. Similarly, under hypnosis, you can be operated on and feel absolutely no pain.
4. Thought rules the world. Man is what he thinks all day long. Have a healthy respect for your thoughts. Your thought is creative. If your thoughts are wise, your actions will be wise.
5. Whatever you think and feel to be true, your subconscious will bring to pass. Your thought and feeling create your destiny.
6. A detective concentrated on one word, 'evidence,' prior to sleep. His subconscious knew that he wanted evidence as to the location of a supply of cocaine and heroin, which he was convinced was being held by three smugglers. In a dream, his subconscious revealed the exact location and he solved his problem. Your subconscious knows only the answer.
7. Many people are clairaudient. Socrates was guided throughout his life by an inner voice in which he had implicit belief. This undoubtedly was an inner voice of his subconscious, which prompted him to do the right thing.
8. A young Japanese student of the laws of mind was about to board an airplane but his inner voice said, 'Don't go.' He

obeyed and the plane was later hijacked. He thereby saved himself from a very painful and frightening experience.

9. You can overcome anxiety by filling your mind with the great eternal truths, which neutralise and obliterate all the negative patterns. Saturate your mind with the truths of the 27th and 91st Psalms and you will find peace and serenity.
10. A woman experienced precognition in her sleep. She saw her husband shot to death. She prayed that God's love, peace and harmony would surround him – that where he was God was. the whole armour of God would surround him. Even though two men aimed directly at him, he was rendered immune to harm. Her prayers saved his life.

If thou canst believe, all things are possible to him that believeth. – Mark 9:23

11

HOW TELEPSYCHICS HELPS BUILD THE MAGIC OF FAITH

Faith is a way of thinking whereby you think from the standpoint of principles and eternal truths. Faith can be looked upon as a constructive mental attitude or as a feeling of confidence and assurance that what you are praying for will come to pass. Faith, Biblically speaking, does not refer to faith in any particular creed, dogma or religious persuasion. Your faith should be in the creative laws of your mind. In your understanding of an Infinite Intelligence (God) in your subconscious mind, responds to your faith and conviction.

Actually, when you stop to think about it, you do everything by faith. If you are a housewife, you bake a cake by faith. You drive your car by the faith in your ability to do so. For example, in learning to drive, you repeated certain thought processes and muscular actions over and over again. After a while the driving became an almost automatic process. There was an automatic reflex action from your subconscious whereby you found yourself driving your car without any conscious effort. In the same way you learned to swim, dance, walk, type and perform many other activities.

You can grow in faith and understanding of the laws of life. If you look around you it is obvious that everything accomplished in this changing world is made visible by faith. The farmer has learned to have faith in the laws of agriculture. The electrician with faith in the principles of electricity has learned all he can about the laws of conductivity and insulation. He is aware that electricity flows from a higher to a lower potential. The chemist has faith in the principles of chemistry but there is no end to his research and discoveries.

His faith caused him to see without eyes

A few weeks ago, a man phoned me and said he was going to a hospital for a serious operation and he said he would like some spiritual phrases to help him. I suggested that he repeat to himself, 'God is guiding the doctors and nurses. God in the midst of me is healing me now. I have absolute faith in the healing power of God.'

After the operation, which was successful, he told me that during surgery he was outside his body and watched the entire operation. His eyes were closed and his body was anesthetised. He heard the doctors and the nurses clearly. The anaesthetist said that his heart had stopped and he received an injection into his heart area, as a nurse massaged his heart. He found himself completely detached from the body and felt that he was no longer a part of it. Suddenly, though, he found himself back in his body. When he awoke he told the doctor everything he had seen and heard.

This man is now in better health than ever before. He said to me, 'I do a better day's work than ever before. I used the prayer you gave me. I have always believed in the healing power of God but never as strongly as since my resurrection from the dead.'

This man no longer has any fear of death, for to all appearances he was physiologically dead; yet he found himself outside his body looking on and was also aware of the presence of long lost relatives. Moreover, he was able to describe and repeat everything said and done by the doctors and nurses. He found himself in the anomalous position of looking down on himself while he was absolutely aware of being completely detached from his body. This experience increased his faith in God, 100 percent.

Everyone has faith in something. The so-called atheist has a basic faith in the laws of nature, in the principles of electricity, chemistry and physics. The atheist is constantly using what he is denying. For example, when he lifts a chair he is using the unseen power that he denies. When he has a problem, whether in mathematics, nuclear physics or medicine, he is always seeking a higher intelligence than his own. No atom or combination of molecules ever gave birth to a sonata, built a Gothic cathedral or wrote a Sermon on the Mount. There is an intangible and invisible Presence and Power which molds the molecules and atoms of the world into shape; but the invisible Intelligence and Power cannot be weighed and measured.

How telepsychics solved a family problem

A man and his wife consulted me about a baffling problem that confronted them. They had received conflicting advice from two lawyers and they disagreed with the advice given by their pastor.

I explained to them about the tendency of an idea to be made visible unless the idea is inhibited and neutralised by a counter idea. I suggested that a passionate desire for a Divine solution with a whole-hearted devotion to right action would find its way to their subconscious mind, which would weigh the question and synthesise the answer in accordance with their request.

The wife's mother was with them, leading a sort of vegetable-like existence that caused much resentment on the part of her husband. The wife's brother and sisters were critical of her because she wanted to put her mother in a suitable rest home and have all the children equally bear the cost, to which the others objected.

After our conference, the husband and wife followed this procedure: They turned their request over to their deeper mind at night, affirming – We surrender to the God-Presence in which she lives, moves and has her being. Infinite Intelligence knows what's best – it also brings about a Divine solution. We have absolute faith in the Infinite grandeur of the Infinite One to take care of this woman, his own child. He gives her freedom, peace and harmony. God knows and God cares, we rest in the conviction that there is a perfect solution.

The first night that they prayed in this way, with a whole souled devotion for a divine and harmonious solution, the sick woman passed on peacefully but not before she had a few lucid moments in which she said to her daughter, 'Your prayer released me.' She then suddenly left for the next dimension.

Your subconscious knows the answer. Listen to its intimations, urgings and promptings. The answer comes to you in many ways.

As you already know, telepsychics deals with your contact with the powers of the Infinite lodged in your subconscious depths. Within your subconscious is the 'I AM' of the Bible– meaning the Presence and Power of God, Pure Being, Self-Originating Spirit – or 'Aum of India, meaning Being, Life, Awareness. Your subconscious is also the law of your life, which, as you know, you can use in either a positive or negative way.

You do not dream with your conscious mind. When you dream, your conscious mind is asleep and is creatively joined to your subconscious. As previously discussed, your subconscious dramatises its contents during sleep. It may present many symbolic pictures and incongruous situations.

Dreams are the television series of your deeper mind. There are all kinds of dreams, including dreams of prevision, in which you see an event before it happens objectively to yourself, members of your family or others. Your dream may reveal the fulfilment of your desire; for instance, if you are very thirsty when you go to sleep, your subconscious may compensate and you will find yourself drinking copious draughts of water to alleviate your thirst. Your dream may also be a warning to avoid a tragedy.

How telepsychics saved his life in a dream

An old friend of mine who carefully reads the 91st Psalm morning and night and who has saturated his subconscious with the truths of this Psalm, believes implicitly what it says:

> *For he shall give his angels* (creative ideas, intimations, promptings, hunches) *charge over thee...They shall bear thee up...lest thou dash thy foot against a stone* (accidents, misfortune or loss of any kind). – Psalm 91:11,12

This man travels a lot in Europe, Asia and South America on government assignments. He was scheduled to go to Peru some time ago and the night prior to his departure, he read in his dream the headlines of a newspaper which told of the loss of 92 passengers with only one survivor. He awoke startled – full of trepidation, with a sense of foreboding. He cancelled his reservation and later found out that the plane went down in the jungles of Peru. There was one lone survivor –the daughter of a missionary – who was rescued by fishermen as she walked along the bank of a river.

This man's tremendous faith and confidence in the invisible wisdom of his subconscious mind undoubtedly saved his life and presented the answer in a vivid, dramatic way, knowing that he would respond accordingly. The reason his subconscious knew about the accident before it happened is that the tragedy had already happened in mind. His subconscious knew about any defects in that plane; it also knew of weather conditions and the state of mind of the pilot, crew and passengers.

Emerson said, 'Nothing happens by chance. Everything is pushed from behind.' There is a mind, a mood or attitude of mind behind everything we do in this world.

The Great Psychic Sea and How to Get Out of It

All of us are in the great psychic sea of mind. Millions believe in accidents, misfortune, tragedies, fires, sickness, disease, crime and resentment and all sorts of negative, destructive thoughts and emotions permeate the mass mind. There is some good in the mass mind, of course but most of it is frightfully negative. Consequently, if we do not keep 'prayed-up' to establish counter convictions against all these fears and false beliefs of the mass mind, these negative emotions will impinge upon the receptive media of our minds. They can reach a point of saturation to precipitate as accidents, misfortunes and various other maladies.

This friend of mine was 'prayed-up'; therefore, he could not be on that plane that was wrecked. Two unlike things repel each other. Harmony and discord do not dwell together. Believe that the love and harmony of God surround you, enfold you and enwrap you. As you continue to commit yourself wholeheartedly to this truth, your subconscious will respond and you will bear a seemingly charmed life.

How his 'invisible partner' retrieved his losses

Recently, I gave some lectures at the Church of Religious Science in Las Vegas, Nevada, conducted by Dr David Howe, an old friend of mine and a former usher in my organisation. One of the members of his organisation told me of an interesting episode in his life, dramatising the power of faith and confidence in God or the Supreme Intelligence residing in the subconscious mind of all of us. He told me that he had been an inveterate gambler some years before and that when he first came to Las Vegas, it was only to gamble. He lost over $200,000 in two nights and on the third night he went broke. He had to wire for money to pay his hotel bill and go home.

Someone gave him a copy of The *Power of Your Subconscious*

Mind,* which he read avidly. He learned that all transactions take place through the mind and that he could not gain or lose except through the mind. Accordingly, in his own way, he affirmed: 'I am mentally and emotionally one with that $225,000 and it comes back to me multiplied in Divine Order.'

He kept the prayers up, knowing that sooner or later concentrated thoughts, passionate desire and focused attention would be registered in his subconscious mind, where they would be incubated and the subconscious, knowing how to bring all things to pass, would synthesise the solution and present it full-blown to his conscious mind.

Three months passed and there was no response. He kept his mental attitude on the beam, however; and one night, in a dream, he was back in Las Vegas at the gambling table and the man at the cashier's window paid him $250,000[§]. All this was a vivid dream. The man at the cashier's window said to him, 'Well, you get more than you lost,' which he ultimately did, as the law of your subconscious is to magnify what you deposit in it.

Following the dream he was transferred by his organisation to Las Vegas. The first night he arrived he went to the gambling table that he had seen in his dream. He recognised the faces of the people at the table and he knew he would win. He seemed to have the touch of Midas that night: everything he played seemed to turn to gold. He won $250,000 and the cashier said the exact same words that he had heard and seen in a dream three months before. His unswerving faith in the powers of the subconscious paid fabulous dividends.

> *I the Lord (your subconscious mind) will make myself known unto him in a vision and will speak unto him in a dream.* – Numbers 12:6

---

*By Dr Joseph Murphy, (Prentice-Hall, Inc. Englewood Cliffs, New Jersey, 1963.)

§Before 1973

POINTS TO REMEMBER...

1. Faith is a way of thinking from where you think from the standpoint of principles and eternal truths. Faith does not refer to creeds, dogmas or religious persuasions of any kind. Your faith should be in the creative laws of your own mind and in the goodness of God in the land of the living.
2. You do everything by faith, such as driving your car, baking a cake, making a telephone call or playing the piano. You developed your faith in riding a bicycle by repeating a certain thought pattern and muscular act over and over again. After a while your subconscious assimilated the pattern, thus enabling you to do it automatically. Some call this second nature, which is the automatic reaction of your subconscious to your conscious thinking and acting. Action and reaction are cosmic and universal.
3. A man believed implicitly that God's healing power would take care of him while he was undergoing a major operation. He found himself outside his own body and saw and heard everything that was taking place. He made a remarkable recovery and now his health is better than it has ever been.
4. Everyone has faith in something. The so-called atheist is constantly using the invisible power he is denying. When he lifts a chair he is using the unseen power and when he thinks, his thought is creative. Whenever you discover the creative power, you have discovered God, for there is only One Creative Power. *The word* (thought expressed) *was God* (or creative) – John 1:1. Stones and molecules do not build cathedrals or compose a sonata and molecular movement did not write the Bibles of the world.
5. A man and his wife had a perplexing problem concerning the wife's mother, who was leading a vegetable-like existence. They prayed with faith and confidence this way: 'We surrender mother to God completely. The Infinite grandeur of the Infinite

One gives her freedom, peace and harmony.' She passed on peacefully in her sleep after she thanked them – a moment of recognition, for praying for her freedom.

6. You dream with your subconscious mind. Dreams are the television series of your deeper mind. A man who had implanted the truths of the God Power in his subconscious mind dreamed of a plane wreck of the ship on which he was scheduled to travel. The plane, which carried 92 passengers, was subsequently lost – only one survivor was found – the daughter of a missionary. This man had experienced a preview of all this. It happened exactly as he had foreseen in his dream. His subconscious had protected him as he recognised the warning and cancelled his reservation on the ill-fated flight.
7. We are all immersed in the great psychic sea of mind, in which billions of people are pouring in all sorts of superstitious thoughts, fears, hates, jealousies, belief in misfortune and sickness etc. Unless we keep 'prayed-up' to establish counter convictions, these negative thoughts and emotions of the mass mind will enter into our mind – do our thinking for us – with negative results. Fill your mind regularly with the truths of God. You will tend to neutralise all the negative vibrations and wavelengths of the mass mind.
8. A man lost $225,000 gambling in Las Vegas. He learned, however, that you cannot gain or lose except through your mind, as all transactions take place in the mind. He affirmed with absolute faith and confidence the response of his subconscious to his request as follows: 'I am mentally and emotionally identified with the $225,000 and it returns to me multiplied in Divine order.' He remained faithful to his assumption and in a vivid dream, it was pointed out to him that he had won $250,000 at the same casino in which he had lost the money. He felt the reality of his dream. When he was transferred to Las Vegas, he went to the same hotel and followed the instructions given in his dream, which paid

him $250,000. The cashier used the exact words that he had heard in his dream.

I the Lord will make myself known unto him in a vision and will speak *unto him in a dream.* – Numbers 12:6

12

HOW TELEPSYCHICS HELPS DIRECT RIGHT DECISIONS

There is a principle of right action in the universe and when your motivation is right and your intention is good and very good, there is no occasion for you to waver or hesitate to make a decision.

As you go through life, you will find that successful men and women in all walks of life possess one outstanding characteristic: the ability to make prompt decisions as well as to persist in carrying them through to completion.

She said she lacked the decision to decide

Recently, during a consultation, a woman said to me, 'I'm all mixed up. I can't and I won't make a decision.' However, she failed to see that she had already made a decision: she had decided not to decide, which meant that she had decided to let the irrational mass mind decide for her.

All of us are immersed in that great psychic sea in which millions of people are constantly pouring their negative thoughts, fears and false beliefs. This woman eventually began to see that if she decided not to decide, the random mind would decide for her in any case, since she refused to govern her own mind.

She began to perceive that there was a guiding principle in her own subconscious mind and that it would respond to her thoughts as she called upon it. that She had to do her own thinking, she realised. Otherwise she was leaving herself wide open for the law of averages – the mass thinking of the race – to make decisions for her.

She reversed her attitude and directed her mind along these lines:

I know that I have the capacity to think, choose and reason things out. I believe in the integrity of my own mental and spiritual processes. I want to do the right thing and whenever I want to make a definite, clear cut decision, I ask myself: 'If I were God, what decision would I make?' I know that when my motive is based on the golden rule as well as goodwill to all, whatever decision I arrive at must be right action.

This woman could not make up her mind whether or not to marry a man who had proposed to her. Following the above prayer, which she recited several times daily, one night in her dreams she saw the man to whom she was engaged swimming in a river, which was very muddy, foreboding, dark and ugly. This dream she realised was her subconscious revealing to her the disturbed personality of the man.

The following day she told him of her dream. Her suitor admitted to her that as he had been diagnosed a paranoid-schizophrenic, he was undergoing psychiatric treatment. He further added that he had suicidal tendencies. They came to a harmonious decision and mutually agreed to break off the relationship.

This young woman discovered that there was a wisdom in her that would respond to her definite conscious mind decisions. She was delighted that she had been able to forestall a tragic error.

You Have the Power to Choose

The power to choose and decide is the foremost quality and the highest prerogative of man. *Choose you this day whom ye will serve* – Joshua 24:15. Begin now to choose what you know to be honest, just, pure and lovely.

> *If there be any virtue and if there be any praise, think on these things.* – Philippians 4:8

His courage to decide transformed his life

A man, aged fifty, lost his position in the firm for which he had worked for many years when it was taken over by another organisation. His associates and friends said to him, 'Tom, you must face the facts of life. You're fifty now and it's very hard to get another position at your age.'

I suggested to him that the first thing he do is cease being influenced by his friends, who had been gloomily telling him that he must face the 'facts of life.' Facts are not permanent; they are subject to change. He began to perceive that his attention should be fixed instead on that which never changes: the intelligence, wisdom and power of the Infinite within him.

I suggested to him that he come to a decision and affirm boldly: 'I am divinely guided to a new position where my talents and experience are appreciated and I have a wonderful income consistent with integrity and justice.' I explained to him that the minute he came to a decision in his conscious mind, his subconscious would respond and open up the way by revealing the plan for the fulfilment of his desire.

A strong urge came upon him to visit another firm handling similar products with which he was familiar. He told the manager of all the wonderful contacts he had and how he could increase the business for the organisation in a wonderful way. He was immediately hired.

When you come to a decision to realise that you have much to offer as well as conclude what you are seeking is always seeking you. When you show an employer or organisation how you can make money or save money for them, you will have no problem getting work. Remember, you are not selling your age or gray hair; you are selling your talents, knowledge, abilities and experience, which you have gathered through the years. Age is not the flight of years; it is the dawn of wisdom.

A good point to remember also is that all the water in the ocean will not sink even a small ship if the water doesn't get inside it. Likewise, all the problems, challenges and difficulties you may have cannot sink you as long as they do not get inside you. It was Shakespeare who said:

Our doubts are traitors
And make us lose the good we oft might win
By fearing to attempt.

From *Measure for Measure* by William Shakespeare

A Simple and Practical Prayer to Make the Right Decision

Remember, there is a universal law of action and reaction. The action is your conscious-mind decision and the reaction is the automatic reaction of your subconscious according to the nature of your decision. Use the following prayer for right action:

I know that the infinite intelligence of my subconscious mind is operating through me, revealing to me what I need to know. I know the answer is within me and it is made known to me now. The infinite intelligence and boundless wisdom of my subconscious make all decisions through me and there is only right action and right decision taking place in my life. I recognise the lead as it comes into my conscious, reasoning mind. It is impossible for me to miss. The answer comes clearly and distinctly. I give thanks for the joy of the answered prayer.

Whenever you are concerned about what to say or do or what decision to make, sit quietly, relax, let go and affirm the above truths slowly, quietly, feelingly and knowingly. Do this about two or three times in a relaxed, peaceful mood and you will receive an impulse or prompting from your deeper mind – a sort of inner silent knowing of the soul, whereby you know that you know. The answer may come as an inner feeling of certitude, a predominant hunch or a spontaneous idea that wells up clearly in your mind.

How his decision saved two lives

The late Dr David Seabury, a famous psychologist, once told me about a friend of his who had been paralysed as a result of two strokes. Once, when this man was alone in the house with two of his grandchildren, a terrible tornado struck the town. The radio in his room warned everybody to go to their cellars, but, because of his condition, he couldn't go to the cellar. Dr Seabury said that his friend began to recite aloud his favourite Biblical quotation, *Be still and know that I am God* – Psalm 46:10. Then he said to himself, 'I am going to save my grandchildren who are asleep in the next room.'

He came to a decision and had an overpowering urge to save their lives at any cost. With herculean effort, he stood up and started to walk. He went into the next room, took the two boys in his arms and carried them down into the cellar. A few minutes later the house was blown away. He succeeded in saving himself and the two grandchildren; moreover, he experienced complete healing and walked for many years after that.

The power to walk was always within this man, lying dormant in his subconscious. In the presence of the emergency, he forgot that he was paralysed when his mind was seized with the idea to save the boys' lives. All the power of the Infinite flowed to the focal point of his attention.

Medical history is replete with thousands of such cases, in which the limitless power of the individual is resurrected in the presence of a great emergency. Man is paralysed in his belief but the Spirit (*God*) within him can't be sick, crippled or paralysed: It is omnipotent, omniscient and omnipresent. The Spirit is the only Presence, Power, Cause and Substance in the universe.

She said, 'I will let God decide for me'

Recently, a woman told me that she would let God decide for her. What she meant by this was a God outside herself, up in the skies somewhere. I explained to her that the only way God or Infinite Intelligence would work for her is through her thought. In order for the Universal to act on the individual plane, It must become the individual. She then realised that God was the Living Spirit within her – that her thought was creative. She realised further that she was here to choose, that she had desire and initiative. This was the basis of her individuality. She finally decided to accept her own Divinity along with the responsibility of making decisions for herself.

Realise the other person does not always know best. Remember, too, when you refuse to make decisions for yourself, you are rejecting your Divinity and you are thinking from the standpoint of weakness and inferiority – in the manner of an underling.

How his decision transformed his life

Some years ago I invited the late Dr Emmett Fox, author of *Sermon on the Mount*, to the Seventh Regiment Armory in New York, of which I am a member. He was interested in the historical displays and the history of the country as it is depicted in the various exhibits in that magnificent building. During dinner, he told me that while he had been working as a civil engineer in England, he had listened to Judge Thomas Troward's lecture on the subconscious in London, which made a profound impression on him.

During one of Troward's lectures, Dr Fox said, I came to a decision. I told to myself, I am going to America and I will speak to thousands.He adhered to that decision. Within a matter of months all doors opened up to him when he found himself in New York, where for many years he lectured to about 5,000 people every Sunday. His decision was registered in his subconscious mind. The wisdom of his deeper mind opened up all doors necessary for the unfolding of his definite, concrete decision.

> *Go thy way; and as thou hast believed, so be it done unto thee.* – Matthew 8:13

POINTS TO REMEMBER

1. There is a principle of right action in the universe. When your motivation is right – in accordance with the universal principle of harmony and goodwill, go ahead and make your decision.
2. The most successful men and women in the world have the capacity to make prompt decisions as well as carry them through to completion.
3. In reality, there is no such thing as indecision. 'Indecision' simply implies that you have decided not to decide, which is foolish. If you do not make up your own mind, others may do it for you; if they do not, the irrational mass mind moves in on you and makes decisions for you. When you are fearful or worried – when you waver, you are not thinking; it is the mass mind thinking in you. True thinking is free from fear because you think from the standpoint of universal principles and eternal truths.
4. When you come to a definite, clear-cut decision in your conscious mind, your subconscious will definitely respond. This may happen in a dream, which will be so vivid and significant that you will have no trouble interpreting it.
5. The power to choose and decide is the foremost quality and the highest prerogative of man.

6. All facts are not permanent; everything is subject to change. Fix your attention and confidence on that which changes not but is the same yesterday, today and forever. The intelligence, wisdom and power of God are constantly available; they never change. If you lose a certain position, there is a wisdom within you that, when called on, will open for you another door in divine order. Remember, what you are seeking is always seeking you.
7. You are not selling your age; rather, you are selling your talents, abilities and wisdom garnered through the years of experience. Age is not the flight of years but the dawn of wisdom.
8. Action and reaction are cosmic and universal. When you come to a clear-cut, definite conscious-mind decision, there will be an automatic response from your subconscious in accordance with the nature of your decision.
9. Often, the answer from your subconscious comes in the form of an inner feeling of certitude, a predominant hunch or a spontaneous idea that wells up from your subliminal mind.
10. Sometimes, in the presence of a great emergency, crisis or shock, man forgets his crippled or paralysed state in order to save the lives of loved ones. When a tornado warning was given, one man, completely paralysed, had an intense desire to save his grandchildren. He walked into their room, grabbed them to take them down into the cellar. All the power of the Infinite flowed to his focal point of attention. He came to the decision that he could carry out his desire – the power of the Infinite responded.
11. When a person says, 'I will let God decide,' he usually means a God outside himself. However, you are an active, decision making, being. You are here to make your own decisions. The Universal will do nothing to you or for you, only *through* you, i.e., through your thoughts, imagery and beliefs. You must make choices – then the infinite intelligence of your

subconscious will respond. Accept your own Divinity; if you refuse, you are rejecting the wisdom and intelligence of the Infinite within you.

12. Dr Emmet Fox decided to go to America to speak to thousands. He adhered to that decision – all doors opened up. In a matter of a few years after that decision, he found himself in New York City where he addressed thousands in accordance with his decision.

13

TELEPSYCHICS AND THE WONDERS OF YOUR SUBCONSCIOUS

The following letter from a woman in New York shows how you can experience the wonderful healing power of your subconscious mind:

Dear Dr Murphy:

You will be interested to know that I used the prayer, Page 106, of the hardcover edition of *Amazing Laws of Cosmic Mind Power** for a cure of glaucoma, which did not respond to the usual eye-drop treatment. In the second line I substituted the words, `re-building my eyes.' It took five months. You can imagine why I like to give away paperback copies of your book every time the subject of illness comes up.

G V
New York

*Dr Joseph Murphy, *Amazing Laws of Cosmic Mind Power* (Parker Publishing Co., Inc., West Nyack, New York, 1965).

This is the prayer taken from of the *Amazing Laws of Cosmic Mind Power*, which she used:

> The Creative Intelligence which made my body is now rebuilding my eyes. The Healing Presence knows how to heal. It is transforming every cell of my body to God's perfect pattern. I hear and see the doctor telling me that I am whole. I have this picture now in my mind. I see him clearly and I hear his voice; he is saying to me, 'You are healed. It is a miracle.' I know that this constructive imagery is going deep down into my subconscious mind, where it is being developed and brought to pass. I know that the Infinite Healing Presence is now restoring me in spite of all sensory evidence to the contrary. I feel this, I believe it. I am now identifying with my aim – perfect health.

You can readily see why she got remarkable results. She persevered, knowing that she was conveying these truths to her subconscious by repetition, faith and expectancy. The healing power of her subconscious mind made her eyes respond according to the nature and content of her prayer.

She prayed for health and her sickness got worse

Yesterday a woman visited me and said that although she had been praying for over a month for perfect health, her condition was gradually getting worse. Her doctor told her that the reason her ulcers would not heal was due to her chronic worry and hostility.

I explained to her that she had to give up her resistance to the healing power within her. She believed that her condition was independent of her mind. However, she was full of ulcerous thoughts of hostility, anger and resentment toward several persons. Actually, she was blocking the healing suggestions of her doctor and also nullifying the effects of his medicine.

She began to understand that her subconscious does not accept idle affirmations but it does accept her conscious mind's beliefs and convictions. Furthermore, she had to forgive herself, for it is much easier to forgive others than it is to forgive oneself.

She decided to cease harbouring negative, destructive thoughts and resolved to substitute God-like thoughts every time negative thoughts came into her mind. She began to pray for the health, happiness and peace of those whom she resented. The point of understanding came when she realised that, if thoughts of hostility, anger and resentment produced ulcers, the reverse would also be true.

She ceased blocking and resisting the healing power and began to discipline her mind by constantly thinking of harmony, peace, love, joy, right action and goodwill to all. She became an open channel for the healing power to restore balance, harmony and perfect health. It is counterproductive to affirm health and harmony and still have a subconscious belief that you can't be healed or to sustain negative and destructive emotions. The healing power and love of the Infinite does not flow through a contaminated mind.

How he discovered the wonders of his subconscious

In *West Magazine* of the *Los Angeles Times*, April 23, 1972, there appeared a fascinating article based on questions and answers by Digby Diehl and Bill Lear [of Lear Jet fame]. At this point, I would like to include some of the more relevant points of this article:

> Beginning as an office boy for Rotary International in Chicago, Lear enhanced his eighth grade education,with a tremendous sense of ingenuity. He used his remarkable subconscious mind into a personal fortune now worth $28 million, 'I have spent my whole life discovering needs and then finding ways to fulfil them I gather a maze of information to pick out the salient things while I discard the unimportant things. I always keep the goal in mind – I insist on solving each problem with the least cost.

'The subconscious plays an important part in this creative process… You've got a subconscious mind that's a computer. You feed in all the information that you can possibly provide. Then, just let it alone and you'll come back in thirty or less days with the answer. They went out unsure but I'll guarantee you they came back with the answer…

One of the unfortunate things about our educational system is that we do not teach our students how to avail themselves of subconscious capabilities. We don't teach them they have a computer, connected with the Infinite that has stored an unlimited number of relatively unimportant details which can be interrelated into the correct answer.

'You use your subconscious constantly without knowing it. It's like forgetting a name and remembering it later. What happened? You fed the information into your subconscious and then you thought of something else but your subconscious said, I've got to work on this and it came out with it. We don't teach students how to do that. We don't even tell them that they have a subconscious… People who believe that they are going to have hard luck have it, because they have set up the mechanics for it. People who believe they're going to have good luck and find the answer usually do find it because they have put the idea of their success into their subconscious. We used to show children how to do this when we taught them to pray. Prayer is another form of feeding instruction to your subconscious….'

These are some of the answers that Bill Lear gave to Digby Diehl. Recently, Bill Lear created a fifty-passenger, non-polluting bus operated by steam; this has served to prove that the internal combustion engine can be replaced.

There are tremendous powers within your subconscious mind. If you are seeking a solution to any problem under the sun, gather all the information you can regarding the solution.

In other words, try and solve it with your conscious mind. When you come up against a stone wall, turn your request over to your subconscious mind with faith and confidence and you will find that it will gather all the necessary data. After synthesising the answer, it will present itself full-blown into your conscious mind.

How he prayed without ceasing

On a recent trip to Mexico I was entertained by some friends. In this particular home, where all of us were talking about the powers of the subconscious mind, one of the men present was an expatriate who had lived in Mexico City for the past twenty years. He told me that over twenty years ago he had had cancer. A doctor in San Francisco had advised him that he had only about three months to live, as the cancer had metastasised throughout his entire system. He had a young daughter about a year old; his wife had deserted him, leaving him alone with the child. The verdict of the doctor was a great shock to him.

Friends advised him to seek treatment in Tijuana, Mexico, where patients in a certain clinic had reportedly been experiencing wonderful results from a unique cancer treatment. He arranged to have his daughter adopted. The agency told him that they would see to it that she was placed in a proper home. After about ten injections at the clinic in Tijuana, he experienced a complete recovery and he has since experienced no recurrence of the illness. Undoubtedly, this man had great belief in the therapy and his subconscious responded accordingly.

Whether the object of your faith be true or false, you will get the same results from your subconscious. It always responds to your deep-seated belief or conviction. In the case of this former cancer patient, it was a blind belief in the efficacy of an extract of apricot injected into him.

After the treatment, he came back to San Francisco and tried to locate his daughter but he could not get any information regarding the people who had adopted her. The agency claimed that, legally, he could not be given the information. He then consulted a friend in San Francisco. She said to him, 'Pray without ceasing and you will find her.' He asked her, 'How?' She told him, 'You love your daughter and you can love without ceasing. You never cease to love your daughter. You don't have to think about her all day long but your love never dies, never sleeps, never wearies. Love will lead you to her.'

When he talked to his subconscious every night, he said, 'Love opens up the way and I meet my child again.' At the end of about a week, he had a very vivid dream. In it he clearly saw his child with her new-found parents. He knew the address in San Francisco, as it was clearly pointed out to him in a dream.

The next day he went there and told the couple who had adopted his child who he was and that he just wanted to see his child again; he explained that he had no intention of trying to take the child from them. He told them of his anguish and panic when he was informed that he had only three months to live. He explained that he had wanted to take care of his child. In his extreme circumstances, he had thought that the only way was to give the child to an adoption centre.

They agreed that the child was too young to understand but they were very kind to him and assured him that he was welcome in their home any time. When the child was old enough she would understand also. He and his daughter now correspond regularly and she has visited him many times in Mexico. He loved without ceasing while his subconscious, which knows all and sees all and has the know-how of accomplishment, opened up the way in divine order. Love never fails.

Telepsychics and Prayer

As previously explained, telepsychics is communicating with your subconscious and getting answers and solutions to problems. The Bible says, *but speak the word only, and, my servant shall be healed.* – Matthew 8:8. A word is a clearly defined thought or conception for good. Healing refers not only to physical healing but to mind, purse, family relations, business and financial conditions pertaining to yourself or another.

Your conscious mind is selective; therefore, do not dwell on doubt, anxiety, criticism etc. The skeptic and the non-believer have a difficult time. The word is your conviction – what you really believe. You do not succeed in prayer by rushing or hurrying or by using mental coercion of any kind. Trying to force your subconscious to do something is like the woman saying, 'I must have this problem solved by Saturday – it's extremely important.'

Instead of being anxious or tense, turn your request over quietly, with faith and confidence, to your subconscious mind, knowing that like the seed you deposit in the ground, which grows after its kind, so will there be an answer to your request according to your desire.

How his child solved his problem

Recently, a man told me that he was about to go bankrupt. He became desperate, realising that his failure would mean loss to many. He asked his child to pray to God for peace and freedom and explained that 'Daddy was in trouble.' Suddenly, out of the blue, friends came to his rescue and solved his financial problem.

His child had told him in advance that an angel had appeared to her in a dream and had told her that her Daddy was taken care of. The child believed implicitly. You must become as a little child when you pray, in the sense that a child is not so critical, analytical or indifferent. Spiritual pride is a great drawback in prayer. Relax, let go, trust your deeper mind and have the faith of a child. You, too, will get an answer.

How a banker uses his subconscious

A banker-friend of mine claims that he solves problems in this way:

I think of the Infinite Presence within me and dwell on the fact that God is Boundless Wisdom, Infinite Power, Infinite Love, Infinite Intelligence and nothing is impossible to the Infinite One. God is taking care of this request and I accept the answer now, this moment. I thank you, Father.

He says this technique of humility and receptivity never fails. Every time a negative thought comes to your mind, laugh at it. Relax mentally.

Speak the word only and my servant shall be healed.

–Matthew 8:8

How to Feel the Joy of the Answered Prayer

Men often claim that they cannot experience a sensation about something that has not been experienced. Well, if I told you that the most wonderful thing happened and yet did not inform you of the details but held you in suspense for several minutes, could you not experience joyous anticipation? Likewise, you can enter into the joy of the answered prayer.

POINTS TO REMEMBER

1. A woman cured herself of glaucoma by claiming, feeling and knowing that the creative intelligence of her subconscious mind, which created her eyes, would heal them. She affirmed frequently: 'The Creative Intelligence that made my body is now rebuilding my eyes.' She also imagined her doctor telling her that a miracle had happened and that she had experienced a complete recovery.
2. A woman got no results praying for health because she harbored resentment, hostility and ill will toward several people. This blocked her healing and she gradually got worse. She decided

to forgive herself for harbouring these obnoxious thoughts and substituted God-like thoughts. At the same time, she poured out blessings to those she resented until she could meet them in her mind and there was no longer any illness.

3. Bill Lear, inventor of the steam-driven bus and many other extraordinary inventions, attributes all his success to his knowledge of the subconscious mind. He studies an engineering or research project from all angles and when he reaches an impasse in his mind and can go no further in solving the problem, he turns his idea over to his subconscious mind, where it gestates in the darkness and gathers all information necessary. When Bill Lear is preoccupied with something else or has forgotten all about it, his subconscious presents him with the answer. He has amassed over $28 million by tapping his subconscious for creative ideas.
4. You pray without ceasing but not by praying all day long. All this means is that you think constructively and lovingly. A man loves his daughter; his love never fails, tires or gets weary. He is busy during the day but whenever he thinks of her, love wells up within him. Love never dies and never grows old; it is eternal. A man whose child was adopted wished to see her again. His subconscious responded to his love and showed him where she was. This led to a joyous reunion.
5. You do not succeed in impregnating the subconscious mind through mental coercion. Relax, let go – just turn your request over with faith and confidence, knowing in your heart that the answer will come.
6. A man about to go bankrupt was panic-stricken and he asked his child to pray for him. The child had absolute faith that God would take care of her father and her subconscious presented her with the answer in the form of a lovely angel, who told her that her father would be protected. Friends came to his aid and he remained solvent. When we pray we must set aside our ego and false pride and accept as true what our

reason and senses deny.

7. A banker solves the most difficult problems by thinking of God from all angles – Boundless Love, Absolute Harmony, Boundless Wisdom, Infinite Intelligence and Universal Power. Then he says to his Higher Self, 'You are taking care of this request and I accept the answer now, this moment.' He gets divine results.
8. If you were travelling in the desert and you were very thirsty, would you not have a joyous anticipation when you saw an oasis in the distance? Likewise, you can get into the joyous feeling that would be yours if you experienced the answer to your prayer now. You would be happy if you wanted to sell your home and a buyer came and paid you the price. Reverse it and the happy feeling that would be yours if you sold it will attract to you the buyer. Action and reaction are equal.

14

THE POWER OF TELEPSYCHICS THAT BRINGS YOU THE GOOD THINGS OF LIFE

Last week I had a conference with a woman who was terribly distraught because her husband had told her that he was leaving her for another woman. She said that after thirty years of marriage this was a great blow to her. I explained to her the meaning of *I am exceedingly joyful in all our tribulation* – Corinthians 7:4. This means that, no matter what happens, you should rejoice that God, the Living Spirit Almighty within your own subconscious mind has something wonderful in store for you. All you have to do is to open your mind and heart and receive the marvellous gift from the depths of your own being.

I suggested also that she 'let go of him' and wish for him all the blessings of life, knowing that divine right action governed him; for true love always frees. I said she must realise that what is right action for him is right action for her. Accordingly, she released her husband completely, whereupon he secured a divorce in Las Vegas. She kept repeating to herself, 'I rejoice and give thanks, for the wonders and blessings of God are operating in my life now.'

As a result of her telepsychic attitude, which simply means her conscious alignment and communication with the wisdom of her subconscious, there was a remarkable response from her ex-husband, who had remarried in the meantime. He gave her an additional $50,000 over and above their legal agreement. Sometime later, the attorney who handled her case proposed to her and they are now happily married. (I had the privilege of performing the ceremony.)

She said to me, 'I know now what telepsychics is: it means to communicate with the Infinite.' This woman realised there was an inner meaning of – *to rejoice in your tribulation*. This does not mean that you rejoice in having pain or sickness or in experiencing a tragedy. Yet, rather, that you rejoice and give thanks because you know there is an Infinite Healing Presence that is always willing to heal and restore your being, provided you open your mind and heart to receive It. Furthermore, you rejoice because you know the will of Infinite life is for a greater measure of freedom, joy, happiness, peace and vitality – in other words, a life more abundant. Life is always seeking to express itself at higher levels through you. Become telepsychic; communicate with the infinite riches in your deeper mind. You will receive a marvellous and wonderful response.

How telepsychics brought success into his life

Some years ago I talked with a man who had a brilliant background but, as he said himself, 'I never seem to get anywhere.' This man didn't know anything about his psyche and how to communicate with it.

I explained to him that there is a definite relationship between a successful life and a person's thought patterns and mental imagery. It is really impossible for any man or woman to be successful unless he identifies himself with success. Success is successful living; it means you are successful in your prayer life, in your relationships with other people, in your chosen work and in your communication with your own psyche.

This man had been identifying himself with confusion, fear and failure for many years. Accordingly, he reversed his mental attitude completely and affirmed frequently:

I am now identified mentally and emotionally with success, harmony, peace and abundance and I know that from this moment forward I am the magnetic centre of attraction that resurrects the powers of my psyche (subconscious) and brings what I affirm into outward manifestation.

He affirmed these truths feelingly, knowingly and meaningfully several times a day. When fear thoughts or thoughts of failure came to him, he would immediately supplant the negative thought with the words 'Success and wealth are mine now.' Whenever negative thoughts hammered at the door of his mind he would reverse them with, 'Success and wealth are mine now.' After awhile these negative thoughts lost all momentum and he became a straight-line thinker, i.e., a constructive thinker – a man who thinks from the standpoint of principles and eternal verities.

In this communication with his own soul, which we call telepsychics, an intense desire came to him to be a teacher of mental and spiritual laws. Today he is a minister teaching the laws of the mind. He loves his work and is an outstanding success in all phases of his life. When he began to communicate in the right way with his psyche, the response came, revealing to him his true place in life and at the same time, opened up all doors for the realisation of his heart's desire.

When you are doing what you love to do, you are happy and successful.

Telepsychics Teaches You that the Law that Binds You Is the Law that Frees You

Think good and good follows; think lack and lack follows. You can use any power in either of two ways. When you dwell consciously on harmony, health, peace, abundance and right action and busy your mind with these thought patterns, you will reap what you sow. On the other hand, if you dwell consciously on failure, lack, limitation or fear, you will experience the results of your negative thinking.

Frequent concentration on God-like thoughts will work miracles in your life. The same wind blows the boat on the rocks or safely into the harbour.

> One ship drives east and another drives west
> It is the self-same wind that blows
> Tis the set of the sails and not the gales
> which tell us the way to go.

Tennyson said, 'More things are wrought by prayer than this world dreams of.' Prayer is a way of thinking; it is a constructive mental attitude with the constant awareness that whatever you impress on your subconscious mind will come forth on the screen of space.

How a boy's telepsychic ability saved his mother's life

A young boy about ten years of age, who listens to my radio program every morning, wrote me a letter saying that every night before he goes to sleep he follows the prayer that I sent him some months ago. It is as follows:

I sleep in peace, I wake in joy. God loves me and my mother and takes care of us. God tells me everything I need to know at all times everywhere.

This boy experienced frequent nightmares but using the above prayer every night eventually healed him of these negative nocturnal occurrences.

His mother was busy preparing dinner in the kitchen for him one day after he had returned from school. Suddenly he rushed into the kitchen, screaming to her loudly: 'Mommy, get out now! There will be an explosion!' His mother glanced at him, saw his ashen countenance and his trembling body and they both rushed out into the yard. Seconds later there was a gas explosion in the kitchen, apparently caused by a leakage somewhere, which partially wrecked that part of the house. The boy had heard an inner voice commanding him to say and do what he did.

This is telepsychics in action. Every night, this boy had been praying that God or Infinite Intelligence, was taking care of him and his mother and that he would be told everything he needed to know at all times. His constant communication with his psyche elicited the response needed to save his mother's life.

How she used telepsychics to eradicate 'the little foxes'

Some months ago I talked with a young woman who had just gone through her fourth divorce. She was full of the two 'little foxes,' namely, resentment and jealousy, which are real mental poisons. Her deep-seated resentment toward her lust husband, whom she had never forgiven, caused her to attract similar types of men, according to the laws of subconscious attraction. Actually, there was no one to blame but herself.

She began to realise that resentment was a negative, destructive emotion generated within herself a psychic pain debilitating her entire organism and having a subconscious pattern of self-destruction. To resent is to avenge oneself.

The other 'little fox' was jealousy, which is a child of fear plus a deep sense of insecurity and inferiority. As is often the case, the explanation can be the cure. She became aware that jealousy consisted of placing another person on a pedestal and demeaning herself. She ceased comparing herself with others and began to realise that she was unique, that there was no one else in the world like her and that she had the capacity to claim what she wanted and her subconscious would validate what she claimed and felt as true within herself.

She prayed as follows:

I surrender all my ex-husbands to God completely and I sincerely with for them all the blessings of life. I know that their good fortune is my good fortune and that their success is my success. I am fully aware that the ship that comes home to my brother comes home to me. I know love and jealousy can't dwell together. I claim regularly and systematically that God's love fills my soul and God's peace floods my mind. I am now attracting a man who harmonises with me in every way and there are mutual love, freedom and respect between us. I forgive myself for harbouring negative thoughts. Whenever the image of any of my ex-husbands comes to my mind, I will supplant the old image with a kindly one, a peaceful image. I know when I have forgiven everyone because when images of former husbands come into my mind, I will feel no rancour. I am at peace.

She reiterated these truths many times a day, knowing that she was thus writing them into her subconscious mind. She experienced an inner and outer transformation and is now married to a wonderful minister and their journey through life has been onward, upward and Godward.

This woman learned that resentment is the link that binds you irrevocably to the person you resent. When you forgive and bless the one that you claim has hurt you, you become free. When your forgiveness is real, the mental picture of the other, when it comes into your mind, will no longer cause you to sizzle – there will be no rancour and you will be at peace. Love and good will cast out…*the little foxes that spoil the vine* – Song of Solomon 2:15.

POINTS TO REMEMBER

1. To rejoice in your tribulation certainly seems paradoxical. All it means, however, is that you know that you turn to the

Indwelling Presence and It will respond to you, heal you, wipe away all tears and set you on the high road to happiness and peace of mind. A woman's husband left her and she began to rejoice that God had something wonderful and marvellous in store for her. As she continued to forgive, she discovered that her ex-husband went out of his way to be generous to her financially and shortly thereafter she attracted to herself the man of her dreams and she is now happily married. She rejoiced in the goodness of God in the land of the living and her telepsychics paid fabulous dividends.

2. It is really impossible for anyone to be successful unless he identifies himself with success. Success is successful living. Saturate your mind with the ideas 'Success and wealth,' and when negative thoughts of failure or fear come into your mind, supplant them immediately with ideas of success and wealth. After awhile your mind will be *conditioned* to success and wealth. By communicating with your psyche in this manner, your true talents and endowments will be revealed and you will be compelled to succeed.
3. The law that binds you is the same law that frees you. Think good and good follows; think negatively and negation follows. If you have impressed your subconscious with the idea of lack, limitation and failure you can immediately reverse the pattern by busying your mind with thoughts of success, prosperity, peace, harmony and right action. You will obliterate the old patterns and your subconscious will free you from your previous bondage.
4. A young boy saved his mother from an explosion in her kitchen. He practiced telepsychics every night by communicating with the wisdom of his subconscious, requesting that the love and intelligence of his deeper mind watch over him and his mother. His subconscious, which knew that there was a gas leak in the kitchen where his mother was working, spoke to him in a strong inner voice and he shouted to his mother

to leave at once, which she did. This is real telepsychics at work. There is that wisdom within you which knows all and sees all and when you ask that It reveal to you whatever you need to know at all times, It will do that and much more.

5. Resentment is the rivet that binds. It is a destructive mental poison that robs you of vitality, enthusiasm and energy. Jealousy is a child of fear and is based on a sense of insecurity and inferiority. A woman indulging in these two 'little foxes' had attracted four husbands, each one progressively worse than the other. Her subconscious psychic pattern of resentment and jealousy had attracted similar types according to the law of attraction. She loosed all four ex-husbands mentally by wishing for them health, happiness and peace, knowing that when she succeeded she could meet them in her mind and be at peace. She succeeded in this mental and spiritual exercise; then she attracted a wonderful man who is spiritually oriented and they have found wonderful happiness. Love and goodwill cast out... *the little foxes that spoil the vine* – Song of Solomon 2:15.

15

HOW TO LET TELEPSYCHICS TRANSFORM YOUR LIFE

The following letter from a radio listener and a reader of one of my most popular books, *The Power of Your Subconscious Mind*,* speaks for itself. The writer of the letter has authorised me to publish his letter, including his name and address:

Los Angeles, CA

Dear Dr Murphy:

About five years ago I began to listen to your radio broadcast, which immediately arrested my attention because you were so bold, emphatic and positive in your statements, many of which were diametrically opposite of what I had been told all fifty years of my life. My life was in chaos, financially, spiritually and domestically; so I reasoned what could I lose

*Dr Joseph Murphy, *The Power of Your Subconscious Mind* (Prentice-Hall, Inc. Englewood Cliffs, New Jersey, 1963.)

by giving your teachings a fair chance.

I began to attend your Sunday morning lectures at the Wilshire Ebell Theater and obtained your book: The Power of Your Subconscious Mind. This book caused me to do a 180-degree turn in most of my thinking. As my thinking changed, so did my circumstances, as, of course, they must.

When I first began attending and reading your lectures, my car was so old, I would park it some distance from the Wilshire Ebell to avoid embarrassment. I did not have a job or position, did not even know what kind of job or position I should look for, my family and I were living in a crowded apartment, on which I was arrears in rent. I was in a fearful, despairing state of mind, not knowing which way to turn.

Well, Dr Murphy, things have *really changed*, so much that I almost am prompted to pinch myself to make sure that all these wonderful things are actually happening to me. And I owe so much to you, for it was your teachings that showed me the right turns to take. I have since read many of your books.

I now have my own business, which I actually enjoy each day as it continues to grow; we own a beautiful, comfortable convenient home, with a beautiful hillside view, my wife and I each have a car of our choice, with all conveniences on each. We have made many new, wonderful friends; all our children (6) are happily married and doing well in the business world. I just don't know what else we could wish for; truly 'My cup runneth over.'

I want to pledge $5.00 per month to your radio ministry, to help enable you to continue to 'tell it like it is.' Thank you from the bottom of my heart and God bless you richly.

Best wishes always,
Louis Menold

P.S. You may use all or part of this testimony in any way you wish, including name and address, which is: 2688 Banbury Pl, Los Angeles, CA. 90065.

How telepsychics works wonders for a builder

A few days ago, I had a most interesting conversation with a builder, who told me that for over a period of thirty years most of his problems were solved through dreams. He talks to his subconscious prior to sleep this way:

> I am going to dream tonight, I will remember my dream in the morning, the solution will be given to me in my dream and the moment the answer comes I will awaken and record it in the pad of paper by my bedside.

This has been his technique for many years. He has received the most extraordinary answers this way. Recently, he wanted a $500,000 loan but all the banks had turned him down. In the dream state an old banker-friend appeared to him and said, 'I will give you the money.' Immediately he awakened and recorded the message and in the morning he called his old friend, whom he had not seen in twenty years. He got the loan without any trouble.

Another time, when he was having some trouble with his son, his mother appeared to him in a dream. She said to him that the boy wanted to become a priest and advised the man to let him do what he wanted to do, as that would heal his frustration. In talking to his son, he found that that was the solution and he has had no further problems with his son.

This builder requested of his subconscious, which knows all, to reveal to him answers in his dream state and since his subconscious is always amenable to suggestion, it responded according to the nature of the suggestion given. The characters appearing in his dreams were simply dramatisations of his subconscious mind, revealing the answers to him in a way that would engage his attention and complete trust. Thus, his dreams have suggested the actions that have been most successful in solving his personal problems.

Begin to Solve Your Problem Now

Before going to sleep, concentrate on the solution to any perplexing problem you have and confidently expect, like the builder, to dream an answer. You will discover that, for what appears to you at first to be an unsolvable problem, a new insight and an answer will be presented to you full-blown in your dream state or when you awaken in the morning.

How she overcame her frustration

Recently, I had a long talk with a woman who said that her mother-in-law 'was driving her crazy'; she kept reiterating this statement like a broken record. I explained to her that her subconscious mind accepted literally what she decreed. If she kept repeating and decreeing that she would go crazy, her subconscious would take it as her request and proceed to bring about abnormal mental states, perhaps bordering on some form of psychosis.

Following my explanation that her mother-in-law had no power whatsoever to disturb her, she reversed her attitude of mind and quietly said to herself:

My body is here in this home but my thoughts and feelings are with the Infinite Presence within me. God is my guide, my counsellor, my way shower, my source and supply. God's peace fills my soul – I am in my own home in Divine Order. I will never again give power to anyone but the Spirit within me, which is God.

She came to the neutral point within her. Whenever she thought of her mother-in-law or whenever the latter passed critical or nasty remarks, she said to herself, 'God is my guide and God thinks, speaks and acts through me. I loosen your hold on me and let you go.'

She practiced this technique for about a week, at the end of which time the mother-in-law simply packed her suitcase and departed for places unknown.

This woman solved the problem in her own mind after reasoning that her mother-in-law was not the cause of her mental and emotional disturbance. This teaches all of us to never give power to people, conditions or circumstances but to give all our allegiance and devotion and loyalty to the One Creative Power within us: the Living Spirit Almighty.

Learn Why Nothing Can Hurt You

Recently, I talked to a congressman who said to me that he had been lied about, vilified and accused of all manner of evil but that he had learned not to let it bother him. He pointed out that he realised it was not the actions or statements of others that mattered but his own reactions to them. In other words, the cause was always the movement of his own thoughts; therefore, he had made it a habit to identify himself immediately with the Divine Presence within him by affirming: 'God's peace floods my mind and heart. God loves me and cares for me.'

He now overcomes all criticism and condemnation by identifying with the God-Self within him. This attitude has long since become a habit. In that way, he has built up immunity to the sharp barbs aimed at him from time to time.

Telepsychics solved his hopeless situation

Following a Sunday lecture at the Wilshire Ebell Theatre, a man asked to speak to me for a few moments. There seemed to be a quiet radiance about him that is, his eyes glowed with an inner light. He told me that, a few weeks before, his two sons had been killed in Vietnam, his wife had died of cancer of the brain, his daughter had died from an overdose of LSD during the long illness of his wife. His assistants in his store had stolen so much that he had to go into bankruptcy.

These were hard blows. He said that he had been in a sort of daze for quite awhile. Finally, his faithful secretary gave him a book, *Miracle of Mind Dynamics*,* which he read avidly, particularly the chapter dealing with the death of loved ones, 'Every End Is a Beginning.' It opened up for him new horizons and a new insight into life. His dazed condition vanished. He experienced a wonderful sense of inner peace; the weight was lifted and he felt a wonderful sense of illumination.

Following the lecture, which was entitled 'Expect the Best in Life,' he proposed to his secretary and she agreed to marry him. A week later, I performed the marriage ceremony.

This man has made his way back into a new and grander life and is now on a special assignment for the Government; he has a marvelous income consistent with his integrity and honesty.

As you can see, no situation is hopeless when you make contact with the Infinite within you.

How he practiced the therapy of words

The late Dr Dan Custer of San Francisco, who lectured on the Science of the Mind for many years in that city and who was an old friend of mine, practiced what he termed the 'therapy of words.' For example, if he felt tense, he would repeat silently the word 'peace' over and over again. When fearful or anxious about something, he would silently affirm, 'Indomitability,' and when an acute problem presented itself, he would say, 'Victory' over and over again.

Dr Custer said that the practice of repeating these words worked magic throughout his life. As he invoked these words, he was actually stirring up the latent powers of his subconscious mind and these powers became active and potent factors in his life.

---

*Dr Joseph Murphy, *Miracle of Mind Dynamics* (Prentice-Hall, Inc., Englewood Cliffs, New Jersey, 1964.)

POINTS TO REMEMBER

1. A woman who had been thinking negatively for fifty years read *The Power of Your Subconscious Mind* and transformed a chaotic life into one of peace and happiness. All phases of her life were transformed as she applied the techniques written therein.
2. You can talk to your subconscious prior to sleep and direct it along these lines: 'I am going to dream tonight. I will remember my dream in the morning; the solution will be given me in my dream and the moment the answer comes I will awaken and record it on the pad of paper by my bedside. 'Your subconscious is amenable to suggestion and you will be amazed at the answers given you. Practice this knowingly, feelingly and with understanding and you will get definite results.
3. Before going to sleep, concentrate on the solution to any perplexing problem; the wisdom of your subconscious will work on the solution while you are asleep and present the answer full-blown to you.
4. Your subconscious accepts what you affirm literally. Another person has no power to disturb you without your mental consent. Your body may be present in the home but your thought can be with God in the midst of you. The other person is not the cause; the cause is your own mind and Spirit. Tune in with the Infinite and think, speak and act from the standpoint of the One, the Beautiful and the Good. Bless your enemies; realise that they are in their true place and claim that you are in your own place in divine order to watch the happy ending.
5. It is not the statements or actions of others that disturb you; it is your reaction to these things. Build up immunity by contemplating the presence of God within you. Make a habit of this and you will develop spiritual antibodies to the

negative thoughts and statements of others.

6. No situation is hopeless. When the death of a loved one takes place, realise that every end is a beginning and rejoice in the loved one's new birthday in God. The 'deceased' are functioning in the fourth dimension of life and they possess new bodies. They are entitled to your love, prayers and blessings on their journey, which knows no end. One man read 'Every End Is a Beginning,' a chapter in *Miracle of Mind Dynamics* His whole life was transformed as he was illumined from On High.
7. You can practice the therapy of words. When fearful, silently affirm, 'Indomitability'; when confused, affirm, 'Peace'; when presented with a problem, affirm 'Victory'; when anxious, affirm 'Tranquillity.' As you repeat these words, you activate the latent power of your subconscious mind and wonders happen in your life.

16

HOW TELEPSYCHICS CAN GIVE YOU THE POWER OF A NEW SELF-IMAGE

Some months ago I flew to Reno at the request of a couple who had been married for twenty years and were now contemplating divorce. In talking to the couple, I found that the wife was in the habit of always belittling her husband. She admitted that she frequently screamed obscenities at him in restaurants and at private social gatherings. His complaint was that she was constantly accusing him of infidelities, all of which were imaginary on her part.

An aggravated case of fits of temper

This woman suffered from extreme outbursts of temper, was intensely jealous and was obstinate in that she refused to admit that she was in any way responsible for the marital conflict. The husband was passive – completely subservient to her moods and tyrannical outbursts. Of course, one would undoubtedly come to the conclusion that for a man to put up with this sort of behaviour on the part of his wife indicates that he must also be partly at fault.

She said that she came from a home in which her mother was dominant – that her mother bossed her father around and cheated on him right and left. She elaborated, 'My mother had no morals. She was cruel and sloppy. My father was a fool, easygoing, blind to what was going on and completely subservient to my mother.'

I explained to her why she was acting the way she was. First of all, she had received no love or real affection as a child. Her mother had probably been jealous of her, making her feel inferior and unwanted. Consequently, for the past twenty years or more she had been building defences against being hurt. Her jealousy stemmed from a sense of fear, insecurity and inferiority. I pointed out to her that her basic problem was that she refused to give love and goodwill.

The Effects of a Frustrated Temper

Her husband had developed ulcers and high blood pressure and suffered from suppressed rage and deep-seated resentment but he was so mousy that he never said a word. He had put up with this chaos in the home for over twenty years.

Both of them began to look inwardly. She suddenly realised unconsciously, she had married a man who allowed himself to be manipulated, henpecked, browbeaten and emasculated. She realised she was completely devoid of real affection. Her possessiveness and intense jealousy of her husband and his female relatives was in reality a craving for the love she had missed in childhood; moreover, she began to see that she had married a father-image.

He finally said, 'I've reached the point where I'm through. My doctor says, 'Get out!' Her constant nagging is making me sick and life is unbearable.'

They agreed, however, that they wanted to make a 'go' of the marriage. The first step was for her to determine to stop doing and saying all the things that hurt and humiliated her husband. He – in turn, agreed to assert his rights, prerogatives and privileges as a man and husband. He was no longer to be mousy or subservient to her tantrums as well as abusive language.

The Mirror Treatment

I gave each one of them what is known as the simplest of all prayers. It is called the 'mirror treatment.' She agreed to stand before the mirror in her bedroom three times a day and affirm boldly as follows:

> I am a child of God. God loves me and cares for me. I radiate love, peace and goodwill to my husband and his relatives. Every time I think of my husband I will affirm, 'I love you and I care for you.' I am joyous, loving, kind and harmonious. I exude more and more of God's love every day.

She committed this to memory. As she repeated this prayer before the mirror, she knew that these truths would be resurrected, as her mind is a mirror reflecting back to her what she holds before it. Perseverance and diligence paid off. At the end of two months, she came to visit me in Beverly Hills. I found a transformed woman – affable, amiable, kind, gentle and bubbling over with new life. Her husband's spiritual prescription was to stand before the mirror twice a day for about five minutes and affirm:

> You are strong, powerful, loving, harmonious, illumined and inspired. You are a tremendous success, happy, prosperous and successful. You love your wife and she loves you. Whenever you think of her you will say, 'I love you and I care for you.' Now there is harmony where discord was, peace where pain was as well as love where hatred was.

The explanation was the cure. This man realised as he affirmed these truths about himself that, even though he might think he was a hypocrite in the beginning, gradually, by repetition, these truths would sink into his subconscious. Because the law of the subconscious is compulsive, both of them were compelled to express what they impressed on their thoughts for that is the law of mind.

How a new self-image was accomplished

I recently talked to a runaway boy, brought to me by his aunt. In discussing his problem, it became obvious that he had an image of an overbearing mother who gave him no love or understanding. As far back as he could remember, from infancy to the age of fifteen, she had exacted obedience through physical punishment and criticism.

At the age of eighteen, this boy was having a lot of trouble with girls. He claimed that he had great difficulty getting along with anybody. His aunt said that she took him into her home, where love and harmony prevail. He seemed to feel envious and jealous of his cousins, who had such a loving father and mother.

I explained to him that his present attitude was simply a defense mechanism that caused him to reject people who were kind and friendly and that it was all due to the traumatic experiences of his childhood. His father had deserted his mother when he was one year old and he had a terrible hatred toward his father, whom he had never seen and who had never communicated with him.

This young man began to comprehend that, undoubtedly, his mother hated herself, because one must hate oneself first before hating anybody else. She was projecting that hatred to her ex-husband, her son and all those close to her.

The cure for the boy was simple. I explained to him that all he had to do was to change his image of his mother. In discussing the laws of mind, he perceived that the image he had of his mother was also his own image of himself, because whatever image he held in his mind would be created by his subconscious and come forth in his own personality.

The technique was as follows: He pictured his mother in his mind's eye as happy, joyous, peaceful and loving. He imagined her to be smiling, radiant and embracing him, saying to him, 'I love you. I am happy you came back.'

After a period of six weeks, I heard from this young man. He is back in Reno with his mother and has been given a wonderful position with an electronics firm. He supplanted the old image of his mother and got rid of the destructive, hateful image. At the same time, he got a new self-image, which transformed his life. Divine love entered into his heart and love dissolved everything unlike itself. Love frees, it gives; it is the spirit of God in action.

The power of a woman's love

The August, 1969, edition of *Fate Magazine* contained the following article:

> In the Spring of 1968 a five-foot, 110 pound woman successfully battled a 1500 pound car for her father's life. Janet K. Stone, aged twenty, is the daughter of Robert H. Stone of Covina, California. He was making repairs on his car when the jack slipped and the car fell on him. Janet heard his cries and found him pinned under the auto. In an incredible upsurge of strength, she lifted the car, freeing her father, then carried him to her own car and drove him to the hospital.

This young daughter's love and her intense desire to save her father's life at all costs, seized her mind and caused the power of the Almighty to respond to her focal point of attention. This enabled her to perform the herculean task that saved her father's life. Remember, all the power of the Infinite is within you, enabling you to do extraordinary things in all walks of life.

He fell in love with a new self-image

During a conversation with an outstanding singer in one of the casinos in Las Vegas, he told me that for several years he had been a waiter but that he had always had an intense desire to sing. Many of his friends who had heard him sing had pointed out to him that he had all the qualities and abilities necessary to become an outstanding singer.

A customer in the restaurant where he worked gave him a book entitled *The Power of Your Subconscious Mind*,* which he read avidly. He said that every night he practiced one of the techniques outlined in the book. He sat quietly for about ten minutes every evening and imagined that he was on the stage, singing to a wonderful audience. He made this mental image vivid and realistic. He imagined the audience applauding him and his friends complimenting him on his wonderful voice. He saw them smiling and felt the naturalness of their imaginary handshakes.

At the end of about three weeks, the opportunity came and a new door of expression opened up for him. He experienced objectively what he had been imagining and feeling subjectively. Love is an emotional attachment and as he began to identify with a greater image of himself, his subconscious responded and the cherished desire of his heart was realised.

The healing power of love

Two years ago I visited a businessman who was very ill in the hospital with 'shingles,' which caused him great pain. He was also suffering from a cardiac attack. It seems that a combination of circumstances had broken him financially and physically. Due to bad investments, he had lost almost all the money he had saved during his lifetime. On top of all this, he had an intense fear of death.

At that time I appealed to his ruling love – that of his fifteen -year-old daughter, his only child. I pressed the point that she was entitled to his love, affection and attention. She needed his

---

*By Dr Joseph Murphy, (Prentice-Hall, Inc., Englewood Cliffs, New Jersey, 1963.)

protection and wanted to be educated in order to find her place in the world. I also emphasised that, inasmuch as he loved his daughter and had to play the role of both father and mother to her (her mother had passed on when she was born), he should now see to it that his daughter would have all the advantages that only loving parents could provide.

I gave him a simple technique, which was to frequently picture himself at home, walking about the house, sitting at his desk, opening mail, answering the phone with the feeling of naturalness, tangibility and solidity of his daughter's embrace in his own home.

I gave him a prayer that he was to repeat with feeling and faith many times during the day: 'Father, I thank thee for the miraculous healing taking place now. God loves me and cares for me.' This man carried out these instructions faithfully. A few weeks later, while still in the hospital and picturing himself at his desk in his home, 'Suddenly, something happened. I felt lifted up out of darkness into a blinding light. I felt Divine love filling my soul. I felt transformed from misery to paradise.'

He made a remarkable recovery and today is happy, joyous and leading a very successful business life. He has recouped his losses and his daughter is in college.

When a person is sick and depressed, it is a good point to appeal to his ruling love and love conquers all.

POINTS TO REMEMBER

1. A jealous person is really sick and suffering from a deep sense of insecurity, fear and inferiority. In many cases, abnormal jealousy may occur when a person receives no real love or affection from the mother or father.
2. A husband and wife seeking divorce after twenty years provided the following information: The husband had high blood pressure and ulcers due to deep-seated rage and resent-

ment. The basic problem with the wife was that she refused to give love and goodwill. The husband allowed himself to be henpecked, manipulated and browbeaten. They agreed to make a 'go' of the marriage, however. The first step was that she would stop doing all the things that humiliated and demeaned her husband. He agreed to assert himself and to cease being subservient to her tantrums. Each practiced the mirror treatment, which is to stand before the mirror and affirm, 'I am happy, joyous, loving, harmonious and kind and I exude more and more of God's love every day.' Each understood that whatever you attach to 'I am' you become. The secret of their success was that whenever the husband or wife thought of each other, immediately he or she was to affirm, 'I love you and I care for you.' By saturating their subconscious mind with the eternal verities, a transformation took place.

3. A teenage boy ran away from an overbearing, cruel mother and found great difficulty in getting along with others. All this was due to the traumatic experiences of his early childhood. The cure was simple: All he had to do was to practice the great law of substitution. He pictured his mother in his mind's eye as happy, joyous, peaceful and loving. He imagined her to be smiling, radiant and embracing him, saying, 'I love you and I am happy you came back.' As he saturated his subconscious with the new image and idea of love, he went home to his mother and there was a joyous reunion. Love casts out everything unlike itself.
4. A young girl, five feet tall, weighing 50 kilograms, lifted a 700 kilogram car, which had fallen on her father. She lifted the car and freed her father, saving his life. The idea to save his life at all costs seized her mind where the power of the Infinite responded. Love works wonders.
5. A waiter in Las Vegas read *The Power of Your Subconscious Mind*, which transformed his life. He had the talent for singing but

he didn't know how to express his gift of song. Regularly and systematically, every night for about ten minutes, he imagined that he was on the stage singing to a wonderful audience. In his imagination he would hear his friends congratulate him. He realised that whatever he dramatised and felt as true in his mind, his subconscious would respond to accordingly. At the end of three weeks a new door opened up for him. He is a marvellous success as a singer today. He fell in love with a greater, grander image of himself.

6. A certain man was broken financially and physically. I appealed to the ruling power of his love for his daughter, which brought about an intense desire to live for her. It helped him overcome his fear of death. Frequently during the day, he pictured himself at home embracing his daughter and seeing the love in her eyes. He felt himself back at his desk doing all the things he would do if he were at home, while at the same time feeling the naturalness and tangibility of the whole scene. His frequent prayer was, 'Father, I thank thee for the miraculous healing taking place now. God loves me and cares for me.' He made a remarkable recovery and recouped his losses and his daughter eventually went to college. God is love and love conquers all.

17

HOW TELEPSYCHICS CAN TAP YOUR SUBCONSCIOUS FOR NEW POWERS

You can receive wonderfully creative ideas and inspiration when you gain a knowledge of the conscious and subconscious aspects of your mind. Your conscious mind, sometimes referred to as the objective mind, is the reasoning, analytical mind. When you go to sleep, your conscious mind is creatively joined to your subconscious mind. Your mind takes complete charge of all the vital processes of the body when you are sound asleep. Your subconscious mind is one with the universal subjective mind and is coexistent with all wisdom and power.

You can learn to tap this universal mind and extract creative ideas and inspiration along all lines.

How to Tap the Telepsychic Energies of Your Subconscious Mind

Your subconscious mind is in contact 24 hours a day with the universal subconscious and this contact is never broken. There is always a flow of creative ideas welling up from your deeper mind to your conscious mind.

I am writing this chapter in the Castaways Hotel in Las Vegas, an enchanting Polynesian holiday resort. Here I have chatted at length with an old friend, Dr David Howe, Minister of Religious Science in Las Vegas.

His technique is to quiet his conscious mind by repeating a Psalm quietly; then, in a passive, psychic, receptive state of mind, he asks for creative ideas to reveal to him the next step in his spiritual progress. Marvellous and wonderful ideas have popped into his conscious mind, enabling him to minister in a far more wonderful way. New wings and greater facilities have been added to the half-million dollar church building that he now occupies and conducts.

Recently, he asked his deeper mind for guidance in planning an ideal vacation. Shortly thereafter, a couple walked into his office to present him with tickets for a first-class voyage for several weeks on a luxury liner. This is one of the many gifts that he and his associates have received through tapping the wisdom of their subconscious minds.

Telepsychics and 'What will I play tomorrow?'

I have talked with many guests in the Castaways Hotel during the last few days but the most notable so far has been a conversation with a man from Dublin, Georgia, whom we shall call Max.

We were talking about the powers of the subconscious mind. He told me that, once a year, he comes to Las Vegas for a few weeks to play what he calls 'the numbers' on the roulette wheel. His technique is to lie on his back, close his eyes and enter into a sleepy, drowsy state. In this drowsy, quiet state he speaks to his subconscious mind as follows: 'Reveal to me the numbers to play tomorrow.'

He told me that he has amazing success, adding that he

discusses his technique with no one but quietly writes down the numbers that come to him in his sleep, keeping a pad and pencil under his pillow. Having commanded his subconscious to alert him to the answers, it awakens him at the right time so that he does not forget the numbers. Last week he made $50,000[$] in one of the largest casinos here and now plans to take his wife and children on a tour of the world.

She asked, 'Should I accept that position?'

I have set aside one day this week while in Nevada to see people who have requested interviews while I am in the city. A young teacher visited me yesterday and wondered whether she should accept a position offered her in a woman's college in the East. I suggested that, prior to sleep, she ask with complete confidence and assurance of her deeper mind the following: 'Reveal to me the answer regarding the position offered in the East. I give thanks for the answer.'

The answer came to her like a flash on awakening the next morning. An inner voice said, 'No.' She said, 'I have a great sense of peace now. I am going to stay where I am.' The answer came from the wisdom of her subconscious mind, which knows all and sees all. When the right answer comes, you are always at peace.

Telepsychics and 'The Question and Answer'

Your subconscious will answer any question but you must ask without any fear or doubt whatsoever and with assurance that the answer will come in divine order through divine love. You can also receive answers during your waking hours. Perhaps you are a businessman seeking a solution or answer to a perplexing situation; perhaps you are a housewife seeking money to pay off the mortgage; or maybe you are an engineer seeking to solve a

[$]Before 1973

most acute problem. Remember, your subconscious knows only the answer.

A Daytime Technique

Many businessmen, as well as professional and scientific men, follow this procedure: Go to a quiet room, be still, relax and think of the infinite intelligence and boundless wisdom within you controlling all your vital forces and governing the entire cosmos with mathematical precision and unfailing accuracy. Close your eyes and focus all your attention on the answer or solution, knowing that the infinite intelligence within you is responsive to your request. Think of nothing but the answer to your question. Continue in this quiet, relaxed, passive state of mind for a few minutes. If you find your mind wandering, bring it back to the contemplation of the answer. If you find the answer does not come in three or four minutes, let go and go on about your business. If the thought of the problem comes to your mind, just say to yourself, 'I have turned my request over and infinite intelligence is taking care of it.'

You will discover that, with this attitude of mind, the answer will come clearly into your conscious mind. Perhaps it will come when you are engaged in some other project or when you are preoccupied with something else but it will come in a moment you expect not and in a manner you know not of.

Telepsychics and Creative Genius

Many eminent scientists, sages, seers, musicians, giants of philosophy and outstanding artists and poets have testified that their discoveries, masterpieces, music and inventions were initiated and guided by intuition, divine inspiration or sudden flashes of illumination.

Thus, many of the world's most creative masterpieces of the

mind, as well as solutions to countless everyday problems, have been achieved through knowledge of and confidence in the powers of the subconscious mind.

Telepsychics could neutralise the so-called 'curse'

I had dinner with an old friend of mine at the Sands here in Las Vegas, which is another beautiful hotel. My friend brought up an old but interesting question about the death of presidents in our country every twenty years. (Many of you will recall the many predictions and statements along these lines during the administrations of Presidents Harding, Franklin Roosevelt and Kennedy.) The prediction, he said, was brought to the attention of the late President Kennedy. It was said that Kennedy remarked that he would disprove it or words to that effect.

My friend brought up the fact that, beginning with President Harrison in 1840, every President elected every twenty years had met with an untimely death. My dinner companion offered the explanation that President Van Buren was so infuriated by his defeat for re-election (in 1840 and in 1848) that he placed a curse on the head of the government for every generation, presumably every twenty years.

An explanation for this 'phenomenon' is quite simple. It may be true that the late President Van Buren uttered the curse or malediction but it is also true that all of us are in the mass mind or the law of averages. This mass mind is mostly negative and impinges on all of us. It often believes in misfortune, chaos, misery and suffering; it can also be full of hate, jealousy, envy and hostility. However, there is good in it also, because millions of people in the world are also praying for peace, harmony, right action etc. but they are by far in the minority. Unless we keep 'prayed up,' we can become victims of this mass mind with its avalanche of sights, sounds, fears or sundry concepts of good and bad.

These tragedies do not have to happen; there is no inexorable fate. Nothing can happen to man unless the mental equivalent is within him; there must be a kindred spirit or predominant subconscious fear that attracts it. Nothing happens except through consciousness. Our consciousness is what we consciously and subconsciously know, believe and accept as true. The Bible says, *No man can come to me, except the Father which hath sent me draw him* – John 6:44. This means that no manifestation or experience comes to any man unless the Father, which is the Creative Power, namely your own thought and feeling, which is the Father of all your experiences, accepts it. We may not know what is in our subconscious mind but we can change it through scientific prayer.

I will fear no evil, for thou art with me . – Psalm 23:4.

The 91st Psalm says:

He that dwelleth in the secret place of the most High shall abide under the shadow of the Almighty.
I will say of the Lord, He is my refuge and my fortress: my God; to him will I trust.
Surely he shall deliver thee from the snare of the fowler and from the noisome pestilence. He shall cover thee with his feathers and under his wings shalt thou trust: his truth shall be thy shield and buckler.
Thou shalt not be afraid for the terror by night; nor the arrow that flieth by day;
Nor for the pestilence that walketh in darkness; nor for the destruction that wasteth at noonday.
A thousand shall fall at thy side and ten thousand at thy right hand; but it shall not come nigh thee.
Only with thine eyes shalt thou behold and see the reward of the wicked.
Because thou hast made the Lord, which is my refuge, even

the most High, thy habitation;
There shall no evil befall thee, neither shall any plague come nigh thy dwelling.
For he shall give his angels charge over thee, to keep thee in all thy ways.

They shall bear thee up in their hands, lest thou dash thy foot against a stone.
Thou shalt tread upon the lion and adder: the young lion and the dragon shalt thou trample under feet.
Because he hath set his love upon me, therefore will I deliver him: I will set him on high, because he hath known my name.
He shall call upon me and I will answer him: I will be with him in trouble; I will deliver him and honour him.
With long life will I satisfy him and show him my salvation.

The presidents who met with untimely deaths could have prevented the tragedies if, instead of brushing the mass-mind belief aside, they had reiterated the great truths of the great Psalm of protection (91st) and also the Psalm of guidance and right action (23rd).

By affirming these great truths you build up an immunity to all harm; moreover, you build up spiritual antibodies in your subconscious which neutralise the beliefs and superstitions of millions of people.

There shall no evil befall thee – Psalm 91:10

If God be for us, who can be against us? – Romans 8:31

The answer to all imprecations, maledictions, mass-mind beliefs, fears and evil predictions regarding assassinations, death, etc., is to keep 'prayed up' by regularly and systematically filling your subconscious with life-giving patterns, thereby neutralising, obliterating and expunging from your subconscious all the negative and fearful patterns lodged therein.

Prayer for protection

Three or four times a day, for several minutes at a time, sit still and affirm:

I am surrounded by the sacred circle of God's eternal love. The whole armour of God surrounds me, enfolds me and enwraps me. I bear a charmed life. The spell of God's love watches over me and I am immunised by the Living Spirit Almighty and God-intoxicated.

This prayer, coupled with the great Psalm of protection, will enable you to go forth with faith and confidence and to be aligned with the Infinite. No evil will befall you or any plague come near your dwelling. You will find yourself in the sacred circle of God's eternal love where you will be invulnerable, invincible and impervious to all harm.

This explanation satisfied my friend. He realised that publications, newspaper stories and commentators predicting deaths of presidents every twenty years caused the masses to fear and believe these predictions. This, in itself, is a frightfully negative force impinging and saturating the minds of millions of people – and according to their belief is it done unto them.

However, a spiritually minded president who knows the law of life could completely neutralise all these dire predictions by keeping 'prayed up'. He could actually laugh at all these superstitions and gloomy forecasts. For he would know that according to his faith he would experience positive results.

She learned to use the I Ching

Among the classics of the Orient, none is more rewarding than the 5000-year-old Book of Changes, known as *I Ching*.*

---

*See *Secrets of the I Ching* by Dr Joseph Murphy (Parker Publishing Company, Inc., West Nyack, NY, 1970.)

The late Professor Carl G Jung wrote a foreword for a translation by Richard Wilhelm in which he stated that he had used it for about a quarter of a century and was amazed by its uncanny accuracy. The *I Ching* is a book of wisdom and when you ask it a question, the spiritual agencies of your subconscious respond with the answer. The most popular method is known as the coin oracle. You throw three coins (pennies) a total of six times, recording heads or tails for each throw and the result gives you a hexagram revealing the answer.

A professional man visited me here in the hotel (let us call him Dr X) and asked me if I would comment on the answer he had received from Secrets of the *I Ching*. He had contemplated making an investment of $100,000 in what seemed to be a lucrative venture but the hexagram he received was 33/Retreat. I suggested to him that the wisdom of his subconscious seeks to protect him in every way and that he should withdraw, which he did.

He called me just this evening, saying that his attorney, at the last minute, had found what he termed 'something shady.' His use of the Secrets of the *I Ching* had saved him $100,000. In answering his question, the Secrets of the *I Ching* answered another personal question, which he had not asked.

In using the *I Ching* translated by Wilhelm/Baynes or the *Secrets of the I Ching*, which is a commentary on the age-old Book of Wisdom, you will find that the *I Ching* has an extraordinary ability to ferret out from your subconscious unasked questions in addition to your particular question, while at the same time revealing the answer and the specific way to handle it.

Telepsychics and the care of the cow

While discussing the Secrets of the *I Ching* with a young lady who had been corresponding with me, she said that a young man had been pressuring her to marry him. The *I Ching* gave her the answer with hexagram 30/ The Clinging, Fire. This hexagram also said that care of the cow brings good fortune. (The cow, in ancient symbolism, means the subconscious mind.)

Actually, she was clinging to a deep-seated resentment and hostility toward a former husband. The fires of hatred and animosity were festering in her subconscious mind. Now the man she had considered marrying, according to her own statement, was an alcoholic and also a dope pusher.

I explained to her that she should take care of the cow and that she was clinging to mental poisons in her subconscious; that is why she attracted this sick man – unconsciously she was looking for punishment. She decided to break off the relationship with the alcoholic and decided to take care of the cow (her subconscious) and eradicate all the negation and bitterness lodged inside her. She decided to forgive herself for harbouring negative, destructive thoughts and she released her former husband by sincerely wishing for him all the blessings of life, knowing that it is impossible to pray and bless another and harbour resentment at the same time.

I explained to her clearly that she would know when she had truly released and forgiven her former husband because she could think of him and would no longer sizzle; the roots of hatred and resentment would be completely withered by Divine love.

This woman is now free. She followed the advice of the *I Ching* and took care of her cow (subconscious mind). It is now a month since I left Las Vegas and she just wrote to me saying that she is marrying a professor.

Let telepsychics work wonders in your life.

POINTS TO REMEMBER

1. Your subconscious mind can give you marvellous new creative ideas when you learn to tap it wisely. Your subconscious mind is one with the universal subjective mind and is co-extensive with all wisdom and power of the Infinite.
2. You tap your subconscious mind by quieting your conscious

mind, relaxing and letting go, then turning your request over to your deeper mind, knowing that the answer will come in Divine order.

3. A man who won $50,000 in Las Vegas used the following technique in getting answers from his subconscious mind: He closed his eyes, relaxed on the bed and entered into a sleepy, drowsy state. Then he spoke to his subconscious as follows: 'Reveal to me the numbers to play tomorrow.' As a result of this practice, every year during his vacation, he visits Las Vegas and often returns with large winnings.
4. A teacher who wondered whether to accept a position offered in another state asked her subconscious prior to sleep to reveal the answer to her. In the morning, on awakening, the answer came as an inner voice of intuition: 'No.' This answer coincided perfectly with the inner, silent knowing of her soul and satisfied her in every way.
5. When you turn over a request to your subconscious, you must do so with confidence and faith that the answer will come. Inevitably you will receive the right answer. When you are active and busy during the day and you seek an answer to an important decision, go somewhere where you can be quiet and read a Psalm, such as the 23rd, which helps to quiet and relax your whole being. Then focus your attention on the solution or answer. If no answer comes in three or four minutes, let go and continue about your business. The answer will come when you are preoccupied with something else and not thinking about it at all.
6. Poets, artists, scientists, musicians, seers and sages have received inspiration, new ideas, inventions and marvellous discoveries by tapping their deeper mind.
7. The mass-mind belief about the death of a president every twenty years, based supposedly on a 'curse' imposed by President Van Buren, could be completely neutralised by a spiritually minded president. All he would have to do would

be to saturate his subconscious with the eternal truths of God. These truths would neutralise and expunge from his deeper mind all the fears, superstitions and negative predictions of the mass mind. For example, any president who filled his subconscious with the life-giving patterns of the 91st Psalm (the great Psalm of protection) would build up an immunity to all the false beliefs and dire forecasts of the mass mind.

8. A wonderful way to develop immunity to all harm is to affirm feelingly, knowingly and believingly the following prayer: 'I am always surrounded by the sacred circle of God's eternal love. The whole armour of God surrounds me, enfolds me and enwraps me. I bear a charmed life. I am immunised with the Living Spirit Almighty and I am God- intoxicated.'
9. The late professor Carl Jung stated that he had used the *I Ching* for about a quarter of a century and was amazed by its uncanny accuracy. A certain Dr X told me that in asking The Secrets of the I Ching a question, he received the answer 'Retreat.' He was about to invest $100,000 in a new venture; instead, he withdrew. His lawyer told him that he saved $100,000.
10. In asking questions of the Secrets of the *I Ching*, which is a commentary on the *I Ching* giving the Biblical and psychological meaning of the hexagrams in everyday language, you will find that it 'will give you answers to unasked questions in addition to answering your particular question.
11. A young man (an alcoholic) was pressuring a young lady to marry him. She received an answer from the Secrets of the *I Ching*, hexagram 30, indicating to her to take care of 'the cow.' The cow is a symbol of the subconscious, which is the source of nourishment and protection. She admitted that she was full of hatred and resentment towards a former husband. These mental poisons were lodged in her subconscious mind. Undoubtedly, this caused her to attract this alcoholic and dope pusher. She broke off the engagement at once. Then

she could surrender her former husband to the Infinite and began to wish for him all the blessings of life. Four weeks have passed since I saw her. Now she is about to marry a college professor. Telepsychics worked wonders for her.

18

TELEPSYCHICS AND YOUR LINK WITH INFINITE KNOWLEDGE

Your thought is your link with the Infinite. It is said that thought rules the world. Ralph Waldo Emerson said: 'Thought is the property of those only who can entertain it.' Thoughts are things. What you feel you attract; what you imagine you become. Emerson also said: 'Man is what he thinks all day long.'

Spirit is God, the capacity of Spirit is to think. This is why it is frequently said by those studying mental and spiritual laws, 'When my thoughts are God's thoughts, God's power is with my thoughts of good.' Remember, God and good are synonymous in all the many Bibles of the world.

Learn to respect your thoughts. Remember that your happiness, success, peace of mind and accomplishments in life are determined by your habitual thinking. Thoughts execute themselves. Your thought is a mental vibration and a definite power. Your actions, expressions and experiences are the result of your habitual thinking. Enthrone in your mind thoughts of peace, harmony, right action, love and goodwill. Your external actions will reveal your inner thought patterns.

When you conceive and ponder the thought, you are releasing its latent power into action. William Shakespeare said: 'Our thoughts are ours; their ends none of our own.' Whatever you think and feel as true, that you will bring into your life. Your thought and feeling create your destiny.

Feeling, insofar as Biblical language is concerned, means a deep interest in something. When you read in Proverbs 23:7, *For as he thinketh in his heart, so is he.* This means that when you are vitally interested and absorbed in music, science, art or your profession, you will be a marvellous success, for the simple reason that you have your heart in your work or assignment in life. You are thinking in depth or feeling the reality of your thought or mental image, which is 'thinking in the heart.'

He said: 'I'm so worried I can't work or sleep'

Recently, a young man came to see me and said, 'Before I got so worried and anxious, I could work all day and feel fine. Now I'm so upset I pull my car over to the side of the road and lie down before I get the power to drive on.'

This young man, about 28 years of age, explained that he was a salesman. He had been to a physician, who gave him tranquilisers but could find nothing organically wrong with him. When the effect of the tranquilisers wore off, he was on edge, jittery, nervous and weak.

I questioned him about his love life. I gathered from his conversation that his attractive fiancée was dating another young man while he was travelling on business out of the city. This was the cause of his anxiety and worry; he was afraid of losing this girl. All of his fatigue and exhaustion were due to his worry and anxiety that he had lost his girl.

I explained to him that doctors have clearly demonstrated through research that stress, strain and worry result in complete exhaustion and debilitation of the organism. At my suggestion, he faced the problem with his fiancée. They had a heart-to-heart talk and resolved the situation between them. As it turned out, she was lonesome and had gone to some local movies with a cousin of hers during the young man's absence.

His usual strength came back and his appearance improved 100 percent. In a few weeks, he married the girl. Divine love had united them.

Telepsychics and her asthmatic attacks

Recently, I spoke at a women's club. During a question-and-answer period, a woman from Trinidad asked me why it was that every time she passed a house of worship, whether it was Protestant, Catholic or Jewish, she immediately got an attack of asthma. I said that there might have been a traumatic episode in her life that was still lodged in her psyche (subconscious mind) – a buried memory – and that the church simply reminded her of the psychic wound.

After a short period of thought, she replied that while she and her family were waiting in church some years previously, a messenger arrived with the information that her fiancé had been killed in a collision. Thereafter, every time she passed a church she was seized with an asthmatic spasm that cleared up a few minutes later.

I suggested that all she had to do was release the man to the Infinite. She had nothing to do with the accident, as she was not in control of his life. Whatever it was in his mind that caused the accident, she certainly was not to blame. Accordingly, every night she affirmed:

I surrender my former finacé to God completely. I radiate love, peace and joy to him. I know his journey is onward, upward and God-ward. Whenever I think of him I will immediately affirm, 'I have released you to God. God be with you.'

I also told her to make it a special point the very next day to go right into the nearest church, saying in her heart, 'Divine love goes before me, making straight, joyous and happy my way. I am going into the church to pray in Divine order and Divine love.'

She followed this prayer technique and also the physical act and was completely healed the next day. Emerson said, 'Do the thing you are afraid to do and the death of fear is certain.' This is exactly what she did and she proved that love casts out fear.

Telepsychics and Objective Thinking

You are thinking in the true sense of the word when you are thinking from the standpoint of universal principles and eternal truths. They never change – are the same yesterday, today and forever. A mathematician thinks from the standpoint of the principles of mathematics and not from the ephemeral opinions of men. You are not truly thinking when you are reacting to the headlines in local newspapers, radio propaganda or from the standpoint of tradition, creed, dogma, environmental conditions or circumstances.

If there is any fear, worry or anxiety in your thoughts, you are not *really thinking*. There is no fear or negation of any kind in true thinking. Fear thoughts result when you make external things causative, which is the big lie. Externals are effects, not causes. The cause is your thought and feeling. Every external condition or circumstance is subject to change.

Whenever any thoughts, ideas or suggestions of any kind come to you, reason things out from the standpoint of the truths that never change and come to a conclusion in your mind as to what is true from the standpoint of spiritual principles.

For example, there is a principle of harmony, none of discord; there is a principle of truth, none of error; there is a principle of life, none of death; there is a principle of love, none of hatred; there is a principle of joy, none of sadness; there is a principle of opulence, none of poverty; there is a principle of health, none of disease; there is a principle of beauty, none of ugliness; there is a principle of right action; none of wrong action; there is a principle of light, none of darkness.

If there were a principle of sickness, no one could be healed. Sickness is abnormal; health is normal. There is a principle of wholeness (health). Because you have the power to choose, you can feed your subconscious with disease-soaked thoughts of fear, worry, resentment, hate etc. However, you then would violate the principles of wholeness, harmony and love. You would inevitably reap the consequences.

Begin now to think for yourself, taking as your spiritual yardstick:

> *Whatsoever things are true, whatsoever things are honest, whatsoever things are just, whatsoever things are pure, whatsoever things are lovely, whatsoever things are of good report; if there be any virtue and if there be any praise, think on these things.* – Philippians 4:8

How telepsychics shows you how to come out of the law of averages

A few weeks ago, I interviewed a young college man who had been associated with a firm for over ten years. He explained that he had never received a promotion or increase in salary, although he had witnessed other men in the organisation with less knowledge of the business and less education steadily move up the ladder with substantial salary increments and added prestige. This man was experiencing and producing according to the law of averages.

The law of averages is simply the mind of the masses of humanity, which, for the most part, believes in failure, lack, limitation and misfortune of all kinds. This mass mind is governed in great part by traditional beliefs; for this reason, it is mostly negative.

This young man was hard on himself. I explained to him clearly that if he did not think for himself, he would automatically be a victim of the mass mind, which impinges on the receptive medium of his mind and does all his thinking for him, resulting in negation, lack with misery of all kinds.

At my suggestion, he began to activate his conscious mind spiritually, which soon became a law of action at his subconscious level. He quickly realised the vast difference between spiritual thinking and average (mass) thinking.

He reiterated these truths several times a day, making sure that he did not subsequently deny what he consciously affirmed:

> Promotion is mine now. Success is mine now. Right action is mine now. Wealth is mine now. By day and by night I am advancing, moving forward, growing and prospering spiritually, mentally, materially, socially and financially. I know that I become what I contemplate. I know and believe that these truths, which I affirm, sink down into my subconscious mind – like seeds, grow after their kind. I water these seeds (ideas) frequently during the day with faith and expectancy. I give thanks for the joy of the answered prayer.

The young man disciplined his thought-life. Whenever thoughts of fear, lack or criticism of self came to his mind, he would supplant the negative thought instantaneously. After awhile, the negative thoughts lost all momentum and today (three months later) he is executive vice-president of the corporation. He realises now that he promoted himself and that his postulates created his destiny.

His trouble was that he thought he should be in jail

A man, about sixty years of age, came to see me one evening. He said that he felt full of guilt and remorse. He had great difficulty sleeping. Two weeks prior to his visit he had phoned me, at which time I sent him to a doctor-friend of mine, an outstanding general physician and a spiritually oriented medical doctor. The doctor told him that his blood pressure was dangerously high – he was in danger of an emotional breakdown. The medicine that the doctor prescribed reduced his blood pressure somewhat and the tranquilisers enabled him to get some sleep. He said to me, 'I need medicine also for my soul, I should be in jail for what I have done.'

This man had previously attended a class I had given on 'Shakespeare in the Light of Mental and Spiritual Laws.' I reminded him that the illness of Lady Macbeth, for example, was her deep feeling of guilt over the murder of Duncan. When the attending physician was asked by Macbeth about her illness, he said:

Not so sick, my lord,
As she is troubled with thick-coming fancies,
That keep her from her rest.

Whereupon Macbeth asked:

Canst thou not minister to a mind
diseas'd,
Pluck from the memory a rooted sorrow,
Raze out the written troubles of the brain.
and with some sweet oblivious antidote
Cleanse the stuff'd bosom of that perilous stuff
Which weighs upon the heart?

The Doctor replied:

Therein the patient must minister to himself. – Macbeth V, 3

Shakespeare, a profound student of the Bible, knew the inner, psychological meanings of all the allegories, parables and cryptic statements in the Bible. He knew that this sense of guilt was driving Lady Macbeth insane and that the attending physician was dealing with a case beyond the reach of any concoction of herbs.

I explained to this man that a good confession on his part would be like the lancing of a suppurating wound, which lets out all the pus and is conducive to healing. He responded by revealing a series of crimes, simply and candidly and removed, as Shakespeare said, 'that perilous stuff which weighs upon the heart.' Guilt had been 'gnawing at his insides.'

I asked him a simple question: 'Would you repeat these acts now?' 'Certainly not,' he replied, 'I am leading a new life now. I am married and my two girls are in college studying to be medical doctors.' I recalled to his attention the fact that physically, mentally, emotionally and spiritually he was not the same man who had committed the crimes. Now, he should cease condemning himself.

The Self-Renewal Process of Body and Mind

Scientists tell us that every eleven months we have a 'new body.' This man had changed his entire mental and emotional outlook on life. He became interested in spiritual truths and began leading an upright life. Therefore, the man who committed all the crimes no longer existed. There was to be no such man anymore.

The Life Principle (God) never punishes or condemns; man condemns and punishes himself by misuse of the laws of mind. When he forgives himself and uses the law righteously through right thinking, right feeling and right action, there is an automatic response of the subconscious mind in accordance with the new mental pattern and the past is forgotten and remembered no more. A new beginning is a new end, for the beginning and the end are the same. Begin a new life with faith, confidence, love and goodwill to all and you know the end will be glorious and wonderful.

Again, to quote Shakespeare: 'Love is not love which alters when it alteration finds' (Sonnet 116). God is love – accordingly, cannot do anything unloving. To feel that you are not already forgiven by Infinite Life is superstition and gross error. Self-condemnation and guilt was this man's illness–and self-forgiveness was his release and cure. One hour's discussion of the truth changed his whole life and today he is happy and healthy.

Woman, where are thine accusers? Hath no man condemned thee?
She said, No man, Lord
Neither do I condemn thee: go. and sin no more.

– John 8:10-11

POINTS TO REMEMBER

1. Your thought is your link with the Infinite. Thought rules the world. Thoughts are things; what you feel you attract, what you imagine you become. Emerson said, 'Man is what he thinks all day long.' Your thought is creative. Have a healthy, reverent respect for your thought, for your thoughts execute themselves.
2. Feeling, insofar as the Bible is concerned, means a deep abiding interest in something. When you are vitally interested in your work or in any particular undertaking, you will be a marvelous success.
3. Worry and anxiety debilitate the entire organism and result in lassitude, exhaustion and depression. One man was suffering from an anxiety neurosis (chronic worry) and insomnia because he was afraid of losing his fiancée. He talked the situation over with her, they resolved their quarrel to get married. He was buoyant and happy once again. Divine love united them and the explanation was the cure.
4. One woman had asthmatic spasms whenever she passed a church. This was due to a psychic trauma that she had not resolved. While she was waiting in a church to be married, she had received word that her fiancé had died in a collision on the way to the ceremony. She released her former fiancé by praying for his peace, harmony, joy and illumination, thereby releasing herself. Then she went boldly into the nearest church, affirming that 'Divine love goes before me and the joy of the Lord is my strength.' She experienced a resurgence

of strength. Do the thing you are afraid to do and the death of fear is certain.

5. True thinking is thinking from the standpoint of universal principles and eternal verities, which never change: they are the same yesterday, today and forever. You are not really thinking when there is any fear, doubt or worry in your thinking. When your thoughts are God-like, God's power is with your thoughts of good. A scientific thinker never gives power to externals or to the phenomenalistic world. He gives power and allegiance to the God-Presence within him, which is supreme and omnipotent.
6. There is a principle of harmony, none of discord; there is a principle of love, none of hatred; there is a principle of joy, none of sadness; there is a principle of truth, none of falsity; there is a principle of health, none of sickness.
7. The law of averages means the habitual thinking of all the people in this world. Most of this thinking is negative. The masses believe in sickness, tragedy, misfortune, calamities and superstitions of all kinds. There is some good in the mass mind, however, due to the constructive thinking of countless others; but, on the whole, the mass mind is very negative. If you do not do your own thinking, the mass mind, with its avalanches of fears, hates, jealousies and morbid supersitions, will move in on you and do your thinking for you. Come out of the mass mind (called the law of averages) and do your own thinking on whatsoever things are true, lovely, noble, dignified, uplifting and God-like.
8. A young man getting nowhere in life began to activate his conscious mind spiritually, which soon became a law of action at his subconscious level. He realised a vast difference between spiritual thinking and average or mass-mind thinking. He claimed as follows: 'Promotion is mine. Success is mine. Right action is mine. Wealth is mine. Abundance is mine.' Whenever negative thoughts came to his mind, he

immediately supplanted them with constructive thoughts of riches, peace, harmony, advancement, victory etc. Through constant discipline of his thoughts, he transformed his life and moved onward and upward along all lines.

9. A man full of guilt and self-condemnation confessed all his crimes freely and candidly and got all the poison out of his soul (subconscious mind). He needed spiritual medicine; for the pills he had been taking, while they reduced his high blood pressure and relieved his tension to some degree, nevertheless could not reach the poison in his subconscious mind. Shakespeare said that in the case of Lady Macbeth, who was full of guilt, 'the patient must minister to himself' in order to cleanse 'that perilous stuff which weighs upon the heart.' This man began leading a good, upright life and I explained to him that he was as good now as if he never had been bad; that he was not the same man mentally, physically, emotionally or spiritually; and that he should cease condemning an innocent man, namely himself. God condemns no man. As far as he was leading a good life now, the past was forgotten – to be remembered no more. This man could not repeat the mistakes of the old – he therefore, was really transformed. He forgave himself to walk out free. One hour saved his life and transformed him along all lines.

Neither do I condemn thee: go and sin no more. – John 8:11

19

HOW TELEPSYCHICS STIMULATES THE LAW OF MIND INTO ACTION

Recently, a woman in great distress came to see me; her husband of fifty years had suddenly turned to drinking excessively and seemed to be on the verge of becoming an alcoholic. She said that several of her religious friends and associates had told her that it was wrong to pray for him because he must first want to abstain by his own initiative.

I explained to her that all this was 'pablum'– it made no sense. I asked her what she thought prayer-therapy meant, then explained to her that it does not imply mental coercion or trying to influence the other person. If she went out on the street and saw a woman collapse there, possibly from a heart attack, wouldn't she call an ambulance and give assistance the best way she could? Actually, I pointed out, she wouldn't have any right not to call an ambulance or do whatever was appropriate for the occasion.

You must remember that pathological sickness, mental aberrations, poverty, alcoholism, dope addiction or ills of any kind do not belong to the Divinity within us, which is forever whole, pure and perfect. It is perfectly right and in divine order to pray for the other fellow, whether he knows about it or not or whether he asks for prayer-therapy or not. To think that you shouldn't pray for your mother, father or friend who is ill simply because they don't ask you to do so is rank superstition.

When you pray for another, you claim that what is true of God is true of the person for whom you pray. You are simply identifying with the Divine Presence in the other and resurrecting the qualities, attributes and aspects of God in your thought and feeling. Since there is only one mind, these dominant qualities in the other are at the same time resurrected in his mind.

How to Pray When You Are Sick

Turn to the indwelling God and remind yourself of His peace, harmony, wholeness, beauty, boundless love and limitless Power. Know that God loves you and cares for you. As you pray in this way, fear will gradually fade away.

Turn your mind to God and His love. Feel and know that there is only one Healing Presence and Power. Undertand this corollary: There is no power to challenge the action of God. Quietly and lovingly affirm that the uplifting, healing, strengthening power of the Healing Presence is flowing through you, making you every bit whole. Know and feel that the harmony, beauty and life of God manifest in you as strength, peace, vitality, beauty, wholeness and right action. Get a clear realisation of this and the damaged heart or other diseased condition will dissolve in the Light of God's love.

Glorify God in your body – I Corinthians 6:20

In praying for someone else, mention his or her name and affirm the same truths for him or her as you would for yourself.

He insisted he was possessed by evil entities

For a great many years, I have counselled and visited with men and women in hospitals in Great Britain and Ireland as well as in this country who have claimed to have been possessed by what they termed evil spirits. Many of these people had what is called multiple obsessions.

The following is a very interesting case of a man about sixty years of age who visited me recently, claiming that he was possessed by several devils who made him do strange things. He had had shock therapy three years previously – had experienced relief for some months – then he said the devils came back to haunt him. They uttered obscenities, imprecations and execrations upon him This compelled him to drunkenness and rape. These so-called evil spirits punched him at night and would not let him sleep, telling him how much they abhorred and detested him.

There were no evil spirits to drive away, I realised. These apparent entities were his own subconscious mind talking back to him. The fact of the matter was that he was full of hatred and resentment toward a former wife, who had run away and married someone else. His vicious and destructive thinking sank down into his subconscious mind, forming 'evil' complexes. He was full of guilt as a result of this hatred, accompanied by fear and apprehension that he had to be punished.

I gave him the 91st Psalm to repeat aloud three or four times a day as also the 27th Psalm to say at night, which is the great antidote to fear. He came to see me once a week for four months and through the prayer process he gradually released his ex-wife, wishing for her all the blessings of life so that he could allow his mind to dwell on her without hatred or resentment.

I explained to him that people seem to talk to us in our dreams and that we also talk at times when sound asleep. If we implant hatred, resentment and hostility in our subconscious, our deeper mind has no alternative but to project these feelings in its own way.

Finally, one night during meditation, I said to myself, 'I am completely fed up with this fellow's belief in evil spirits. He is just talking to himself and I know it. There is only One Spirit (God), the Everlasting One, the All Wise One and the All Knowing One only one Divine Mind. This man is now aware of what I am aware. He feels God's love in his heart right now.'

The next day, when he came to see me, he said, 'A strange thing happened last night. Jesus appeared to me and said, 'These evil spirits are not real; they are in your own mind and you are now free.' This man was completely healed.

During our many consultations, I finally had to bring myself to the point of subconscious conviction, which obliterated his belief out of my mind. It wasn't just the mentally disordered man who had to be cleansed of his false beliefs; it was also I who had to be cleansed and healed. I believe this is true in all prayer-therapy, whether the counsellor is aware of it or not.

When I reached a clear-cut decision and conviction in my mind about these nonsensical and apparently evil entities in his mind, my belief was communicated to him instantaneously. There being but one mind, wholeness and peace were resurrected in his mind.

Her psychic experience revealed hidden wealth

A young secretary who attends my lectures at the Wilshire Ebell Theatre every Sunday morning said to me a few days ago that, every night for about a week, she had experienced a vivid dream wherein she had a spade in her hand and was digging up the earth in the backyard of her home. She said that she felt quite elated after each dream She wanted to know what I thought about this.

I explained to her that a dream is always very personal and that it could possibly mean that she should dig up out of herself some hidden treasure, such as a talent. If that did not ring a bell in her heart, she should get her brother or father to dig up the backyard. She asked her father to do this and he agreed, rather reluctantly. To their amazement, he dug up an old earthenware jug full of gold coins dating back to 1898.

The value of the coins ran into thousands of dollars and

enabled her to finish college, buy a Rolls Royce, which she had always wanted. There was enough left over to fill the needs of all the family. This young woman, who had been praying for prosperity and a way to complete her college education, found her wishes embodied in her dreams.

Telepsychics banished her frustration

A widow with two sons was praying that she would attract a marriage partner who would harmonise with herself and the boys and be a wonderful father to them. She had frequent dreams. In almost every dream she missed the bus and was late to her office every day, yet objectively she was always on time. I asked her whether there was anyone in her office who appealed to her as a future husband. She replied that the Assistant Vice President had asked her out to a show and dinner several times but that she had refused because she thought that it was not good policy and that it was frowned upon by the hierarchy of her particular firm.

I told her that I felt her prayer was answered but that she was undoubtedly missing a wonderful opportunity for marriage. Her subconscious mind was prompting her symbolically to take advantage of the opportunity. Moreover, a bus is a symbol of sex, which is a part of the marriage act. She went to work the next day quite enthused and told the Assistant Vice President that she would be delighted to accept his invitation of a few days ago because of a change of circumstances. In a few weeks they were happily married and he was indeed the right man for her and the boys.

Actually, this widow had been rejecting the answer to her prayer, so her subconscious had no alternative but to speak to her in a dream.

> *I the Lord (subconscious mind) will make myself known unto him in a vision and will speak unto him in a dream.*
>
> – Numbers 12:6

Let the Law of Attraction Work for You

Your thoughts have their affinities. As Marcus Aurelius, the great Roman emperor and philosopher, said, 'Our life is what our thoughts make it.' Your dominant thought underlies all your other thoughts and colors them in the same way a small amount of indigo dye colors the entire contents of a five-gallon demijohn of water. William James, the father of American psychology, said, 'The greatest discovery of my generation is that human beings can alter their lives by altering their attitudes of mind.'

In talking to a beautiful young woman today, who was talented, charming, vivacious and highly educated, I discovered that she was actually ruining her life by her vicious, destructive, hateful patterns of thought. She started on a tirade against her father, who was deceased. In addition, she was full of hatred toward her mother. She had lost three positions in the course of a year, due, as she said, to her sarcastic and biting tongue. She was poisoning herself emotionally and her physical being was also disturbed, necessitating a hysterectomy and an operation for an ulcer.

I explained to this young lady that the whole world was before her. She could start from today itself to prove to herself that her whole world, that is, her body, conditions, circumstances, social and financial life would magically melt in the image and likeness of her habitual thinking.

She agreed to change her thoughts and to keep them changed. Whenever a negative thought came to her mind, she would immediately supplant it with thoughts of love and goodwill. She understood that by supplanting the negative thoughts regularly and systematically, she would succeed in breaking the spasm of destructive thinking that was ruining her life.

An Effective Affirmation

I gave her the following affirmation to use frequently, knowing that by reiteration of these truths and feeling the reality of what she affirmed, these truths would sink into her subconscious and since the law of the subconscious is compulsive, she would be compelled to ways of pleasantness and paths of peace. I was sure that from that point on her journey would be onward, upward and God-ward:

The gifts of God are mine now. I live in the Presence of God, from whom all blessings flow. I use every moment of this day to glorify God. God's harmony, peace and abundance are mine now. Divine love flowing from me blesses all who come into my atmosphere. God's love is felt by all present here and His love is healing them now.

I fear no evil for God is with me. I am always surrounded by the sacred circle of God's love and power. I claim, feel, know and believe definitely and positively that the spell of God's love and eternal watchfulness guides, heals and watches over me and all members of my family.

I forgive everyone and I sincerely radiate God's love, peace and goodwill to all men everywhere. At the center of my being is peace; this is the peace of God. In this stillness I feel His strength, guidance and the love of His Holy Presence. I am divinely guided in all my ways. I am a clear channel for God's love, light, truth and beauty. I feel His River of Peace flowing through me now. I know that all my problems are dissolved in the mind of God. God's ways are my ways. The words I have spoken accomplish that whereunto they are sent. I rejoice and give thanks, realising my prayers are answered.

It is so.

Telepsychic Materialisations Are Real as Phenomena

In discussing telepsychics, which deals with the wonder-working powers of your subconscious mind, I am frequently asked by great numbers of people what I think about the materialisations in séances. First of all, I believe that the so-called control of a medium is simply a dominant idea in the subconscious mind. We must accept the fact that psychic phenomena exist. Your subconscious possesses clairvoyant, clairaudient and telekinetic powers, which are faculties of the mind in all of us.

Some years ago, Dr Evelyn Fleet, of Caxton Hall, London. and a retired colonel-friend of hers took me to a mediumistic séance in London, where we witnessed eight materialisations as solid as our own bodies. Her colonel-friend was a retired Army doctor and he examined the materialisations and tested their pulse and blood pressure, checked their teeth and cut off pieces of their hair.

Each materialisation weighed as much as one of the three of us. We talked with them and afterwards, Dr Fleet thought that the woman with whom she had been speaking might have been her mother; but she wasn't sure. We received fairly intelligent answers from them and one resembled the colonel's sister, who had passed on some years before.

All this took place without any blackout of lights. The medium was in a trance state. All of the men wore suits and the women had on dresses. There was no chicanery or trickery; these materialisations were not illusions. An illusion can't be demonstrated as having flesh and blood, hair, clothes, vocal organs and pulse. An illusion is something that deceives by producing a false impression: a state or condition of being deceived. All of the materialisations were apparently real but I do not believe one of the women was Dr Fleet's mother or another the colonel's sister.

All of them were real as phenomena or manifestations or projections of the ectoplasmic substance of the medium, which is capable of projecting the thought patterns of relatives in the subconscious of those present, thus giving them flesh and blood and the capacity to speak, act and give appropriate answers to questions. I believe all the materialisations were dramatisations of the subconscious of the medium.

Dr Fleet sent the hair that was cut by her friend from the

woman she thought might be her mother and the chemical laboratory said that it could not be analysed; it was of 'unknown origin.' A few days later, the laboratory said the hair had dissolved and no traces were left!

Dr Fleet agreed with me that it would be rather naive to think that you could walk into a séance to call forth friends or loved ones from the next dimension. Then just have them appear in a few minutes in response to your request. All your loved ones are functioning in fourth-dimensional bodies, in the many mansions of our Father's house. They are moving onward and upward, going from glory to glory, on that journey that knows no end.

POINTS TO REMEMBER

1. It is superstition to think that you should not pray for another who is an alcoholic or who has cancer or any other ailment. If someone had an accident, wouldn't you call an ambulance or give help to the best of your ability? Prayer therapy is not coercion. Prayer is claiming that what is true of God is true of the other person. The divine nature is within every person. It is the divine will that this be expressed in all men and women.
2. When you pray for a sick person, never dwell on symptoms, pains or aches. Quietly claim that the uplifting, healing, strengthening power of the Healing Presence is flowing through the loved one, making him whole and perfect.
3. The devils that plague man and cause multiple obsessions are hate, jealousy, envy, malice, guilt and self-condemnation. When these mental gangsters take charge of our mind, we lose all reasoning power and become victims of our own vicious and destructive thinking. When a man hears voices telling him to do destructive things, it is his own subconscious talking back to him. In other words, he is talking to himself. Gradually, one man came to see that it was his own

subconscious mind responding to his destructive thinking that was moving him. As I cleansed my mind of all this nonsense with the realisation that there is only One Spirit and One Power and at the same time claimed that this man was now aware of what I am aware, he was healed.

4. Many times your dreams reveal answers to your most perplexing problems. A young woman had a recurrent dream wherein she was digging up her backyard. She had been praying for prosperity. At my suggestion, she got her father to dig up the garden, where they found a jar full of old gold coins worth a small fortune.
5. A widow seeking to remarry stated that she frequently had a vivid dream in which she always missed the bus and was late for work; yet objectively she was always on time. She realised that she was missing the opportunity to marry by rejecting the invitation of one of the managers in her office. She accepted his invitation and marriage resulted, which was the perfect answer to her prayer.
6. Marcus Aurelius said, 'Our life is what our thoughts make it.' Emerson said, 'A man is what he thinks all day long.' Your dominant thought underlies and colors all your other thoughts. A young woman was destroying her life by hateful, vengeful thoughts directed at her parents and others. She experienced ill health. As a result of this, she had to undergo two serious operations. She reversed her thinking and decided to supplant all negative thoughts instantaneously with God-like, loving thoughts. As she made a habit of this, her whole world magically melted into the image, to present the likeness of her contemplation. She became what she contemplated.
7. Many people ask me about materialisations in seances, in which people appear, speak, walk around and converse with you. The phenomena are real but they are only apparently real. They are not your loved ones, as they are functioning in the next dimension of life, moving onward, upward and

Godward. They are separated from you by frequency only. When you cut a piece of hair from one of these materialisations, it can't be tested in a laboratory, as it is an unknown substance. The medium, in a trance state, can tap images of your loved ones to bring about ectoplasmic projections and forms of men and women who have normal pulse rates and other manifestations of life.

20

HOW TELEPSYCHICS SHARPENS THE POWERS OF YOUR MIND

Your subconscious mind is the builder and rebuilder of your body, having control over all of its so-called involuntary functions. It governs respiration, digestion, assimilation, circulation, elimination and all other automatic activities. The subconscious is also a wonderful chemist, transmuting all the food you eat into tissue, muscle, bone, blood and hair to constantly building new cellular structures.

Your subconscious is also the storehouse of memory. Whatever your conscious mind really believes and accepts as true, your subconscious will bring to pass. Because your deeper mind is amenable to suggestion, it is also the seat of habit.

In hypnotic experiments, your subconscious accepts all suggestions given and reasons deductively only. Its deductions are always in harmony with premises; therefore, all suggestions should be life-giving and constructive in quality.

The language of your subconscious is symbolic. This is indicated in your dreams, which often dramatise your unfulfilled or repressed desires. Your subconscious is a wonderful impersonator; it will impersonate whatever is vividly suggested. As the seat of all psychic experiences, it perceives intuitively, independent of time and space. You must remember also that within your subconscious is the super conscious (called the great Oversoul by Emerson) or the Presence of God or Supreme Intelligence. In other words, the I AM or the Living Spirit Almighty, is within you, which knows all and sees all. Within your subconscious is Infinite Wisdom, Infinite Love and all the qualities and attributes of the Infinite Being called God.

Your conscious mind recognises and understands the outer world through the medium of the five senses: it reasons by induction, deduction, analysis and analogy. You choose, select, plan and initiate with your conscious mind, which acts as the seat of will. Your will is made up of desire, decision and determination.

You concentrate with your conscious mind. Through your focused attention, you impress your subconscious mind. Because you imagine and make mental pictures with your conscious mind, you can impregnate your subconscious more effectively by clearly visualising what you wish to be, to do and to have. Your conscious mind can decree success and prosperity through its power of conscious control in constructive thinking, speaking and imagining. You can saturate your subconscious with the idea of abundance and success.

Emergencies as Stimulators of Mental Powers

Your conscious mind becomes highly receptive to your subconscious during emergencies, at which time the wisdom and intelligence of your subconscious take control. Your conscious mind plays a receptive role to the subconscious in psychic phenomena. Your conscious mind may be illumined and inspired by calling on the wisdom and intelligence of your deeper mind, which knows all and sees all.

I have visited the late Geraldine Cummins, at her homes in London, England and Cork, Ireland, several times. (She is the author of *Unseen Adventures, The Scripts of Cleophas and* many other books.) She has been investigated by some of the foremost scientists in England, all of whom have testified to her remarkable psychic powers.

I had many sittings with her, as I was always interested in extrasensory perception and psychic phenomena of all kinds. In these sessions, Miss Cummins would become very quiet and enter into a passive, receptive, psychic state. Her conscious mind was partially submerged. Suddenly she claimed that her control 'Astor' had taken over and she would begin to write, automatically, page after page of extraordinary information.

In one instance, she said that my sister, Mary Agnes, who had passed on, was communicating. On reading the pages, I discovered that many paragraphs were in Gaelic, some in French and some in Latin – languages which Geraldine did not speak. Also, in the writing, my sister pointed out six instances by which I would recognise her, all of which were extraordinarily accurate. She went over our childhood and covered intimate details and made many prophetic statements, all of which subsequently came to pass.

In this instance, I think Geraldine was simply an amanuensis, writing down events of which she actually knew nothing. When Geraldine finished writing, she had no idea whatever of what she had written. In this instance, the evidence seemed overwhelming. I do believe it was my sister in the next dimension actually communicating.

Normal psychic power

There are many psychics who can tap the contents of your mind while they are in a normal state, i.e., they are in a perfectly conscious state of mentality. This capacity is within everyone but some have it developed to a greater extent than others.

Abnormal psychic powers

Geraldine Cummins invited me to a séance conducted by a friend of hers in the South of Ireland. This particular Irish medium entered into a full trance and claimed that she was controlled by an Egyptian priest. In this state, she revealed wonderful hidden powers. Six of us sat on a table, for example and it was lifted up easily by the medium's subconscious mind.

One professor who was present was convinced that his mother spoke to him. He claimed that it was her voice and her mannerisms and that she referred to him by his pet name and spoke to him in Greek, her native tongue, a language which the entranced medium did not understand.

Many materialised forms appeared, some of whom spoke. All were dressed and had all their human faculties. One woman present chatted with a young materialised girl whom she claimed to be her daughter. These materialisations lasted about five or six minutes and then vanished. All this took place in the afternoon – not under dim lights but in full view of all those present. The forms were, in all probability, ectoplasmic projections of the medium.

How she psychometrises

Recently, Dr David Howe of Las Vegas introduced me to a psychometrist, who has the extraordinary ability to read the subjective side of things. By touching a ring belonging to a person or a letter he has written, she can give a complete description of the person: his characteristics, tendencies, type of work, age, background and also his future. When she touches a ring worn by the subject in question, she feels a certain vibration and enters into the mental atmosphere of the person. The reason for this is that the subjective mind permeates and penetrates all things. The man's ring is impregnated with his mental atmosphere, enabling the medium to enter his innermost thoughts, beliefs and experiences.

Telepsychics and Inner Voices

Last year, during a seminar on the sea, one of the ship's officers with whom I had dinner said that from time to time, particularly if there was anything wrong with the ship, he heard inner voices silently speaking to him, telling him exactly where the trouble was and also what to do about it. He realised that he had a remarkable ability, which others of the crew did not possess and said that, in most cases, it came to him as a warning.

One time on board ship off the coast of Italy while he was in his cabin, the inner voice said to him that a member of the crew (giving the name of the man) was coming down to shoot him. The crew member was going berserk. The officer said, 'I locked my door, called the captain and had the crewman locked up and when we got to port, he was committed to an asylum.' The inner voice was 100 percent correct, as this man was armed with a pistol. He subsequently confessed that he was there to murder the ship's officer.

These warnings can also come in dreams and visions of the night.

The captain's inner voice was real, because he made it a habit to instruct his subconscious that the voice would be to protect, heal and bless him in all ways, i.e., it would be the voice of his Higher Self. He constantly reiterated that all monitions, promptings and inner instructions would come from the Infinite Presence within his subconscious mind.

Conversing with Voices in Séance Rooms

During many séances, which I have attended in London, Johannesburg, Cape Town and New York City, with the medium in a trance state, voices of discarnate entities or disembodied spirits have seemingly filled the air. I have conversed at length with some of these voices and have received extraordinarily intelligent answers. I have heard others present at these séances – some of them physicists, medical doctors and college professors – openly say that they were definitely conversing with former colleagues or loved ones. All this was based upon the professional background, tone of voice, characteristics, mannerisms, peculiarities and idiosyncrasies of those who were functioning in the fourth-dimension.

Personally, insofar as those who declared to be relatives of mine, I was not completely satisfied in every instance as to whether the voices were caused by the subjective mind of the medium or whether they were actually the voices of loved ones in the next dimension of life.

It is, however, a thrilling, fascinating and enthralling experience. In one particular instance, I believe I heard the voice of my father, who spoke four languages – ancient Gaelic, English, French and Latin. His voice was natural, just the same as if he were in the room. He said to me, 'Joe, you will know it is your father by what I am saying. I taught you this prayer when you were five years old.' Then he repeated the Lord's Prayer in Gaelic, in French and in Latin. He asked to be introduced to all present, as he said he didn't recognise any of them. He covered many incidents in my early life that I had forgotten; these incidents were subsequently verified by my sister, who is still alive on this plane.

One might say that the medium was tapping my subconscious and was thus able to impersonate my father and mimic his voice; but that is rather far-fetched in this instance. You could hypnotise a man – tell him he is now your brother. Yet never having met your brother, he could not imitate his voice, mannerisms and gestures nor could he dramatise his personality.

She saw her mother before she passed on

A young schoolteacher who comes to my lectures on Sundays told me that, one day during lunch hour at school, she was alone arranging things in the schoolroom for the next session and suddenly, her mother appeared to her and said, 'Good bye,' and vanished.

This type of apparition is not at all uncommon. Undoubtedly, her mother, who was living in New York City, was thinking of her daughter prior to her transition and projected her personality to her daughter. In checking the time difference, she found out that her mother had appeared to her at the exact moment she had expired.

The ghost gave him a message and disappeared

The late Geraldine Cummins introduced me to a man in her home in London, mentioning the fact that he felt that his home was haunted because he frequently heard loud footsteps coming up the stairs in the home. Once his maid saw the apparition and was so frightened, actually petrified with fear, that she was completely immobilised for a few minutes after the experience. The maid refused to stay and left the next morning.

I suggested to him that the so-called ghost could well be a thought-form, probably of someone in the house who had met with foul play. A person who had an intense desire to let someone know what had happened prior to death. This intense desire often takes the form of the person but the moment it gives the message, the thought-form is dissipated. I urged him, the moment he heard the footsteps, to go and meet the so-called ghost. Ask for the message and then listen, which is exactly what he did. He saw the apparition one evening and he said, 'Give me your message,' and the story of his murder by his brother was given – immediately the form disappeared.

A thought-form is not the personality of the man; it is the word or thought-form sent forth and it remains for hundreds of years, until someone receives the message.

The Bible says:

> *So shall my word be that goeth forth out of my mouth: it shall not return unto me void but it shall accomplish that which I please and it shall prosper in the thing whereto I sent it.* – Isaiah 55:11

In the case of the apparition, the word was the thought and intense desire to communicate to someone how he had met his untimely death .the word (thought-form) remained hovering around until this man challenged it and listened. Subsequently, he told me that it was verified that a man had been murdered in that house and that the culprit had never been apprehended.

She said: 'They are practicing black magic against me'

Black magic, sorcery and devil-worship have been taught and practiced from time immemorial. Actually, the whole idea of sorcery is based on gross ignorance; all it means is thinking negatively of another person and wishing him evil. To think evil of another is to think evil of yourself. What you wish for another you are actually wishing for yourself.

The office girl who used the term 'black magic' said to me that one of the girls in the office had told her confidentially that several of the girls were practicing voodoo against her by praying that she pass out of the body. This frightened her. I explained to her that their prayers were null and void and that all she had to do was to affirm:

> I am alive with the Life of God. God is Life and that is my Life now. God's Love fills my soul. His Love surrounds me, enfolds me and enwraps me and I bear a charmed life. The spell of God envelopes me at all times.

I explained to her that she should commit the above prayer to memory and affirm these truths frequently, as frequent habitation of the mind with these truths would cast out fear. Whenever the thought of voodoo or black magic came to her, all she had to do was supplant the thought with, 'God loves and cares for me.' I pointed out that Spirit (God) is one and indivisible. One part of Spirit can't be antagonistic to another part of Spirit. In other words, Spirit can't be divided against Itself. This truth is final, absolute and eternal. This simple universal truth neutralises and obliterates the question of black magic, sorcery as well as malicious malpractice for all time.

She saw the light and faithfully followed my instructions and a strange thing happened. The three girls who were believed to have been wishing her injury were all killed in an accident on the way to work. The evil that they had been projecting to this girl undoubtedly boomeranged on themselves, because it had no place to go; so their negative or malicious thinking returned in a magnified way to themselves. Thus, they actually destroyed themselves.

There are people in many parts of the world who try to use their mental powers to hurt others but anyone who understands his alignment with the Infinite can't be affected by their manipulations. People who practice what they call voodoo, malpractice or black magic really have no power. They are using suggestion, which is a power but not the power. The Power is Almighty and moves as unity, harmony, beauty, love and peace.

Whatever name you give it – whether it be Satan, black magic, sorcery or malicious malpractice – all these things are simply negative suggestions. Refuse to give power to the suggestions of others. Give power to the Only Presence and Power. Read the 91st Psalm and believe it and you will lead a charmed life.

She wrote answers on paper without pen or pencil

Recently, I was a guest in the home of an old friend of mine in Mexico City. There was a very beautiful woman present who practiced automatic writing. She held a pen in her hand and suddenly her hand was controlled by her own subconscious mind. She said that her hand was controlled by a discarnate entity called

Dr Latella, presumably a former Spanish medical doctor.

She brought forth wonderful messages for all those present (eight altogether) and all agreed that everything she had written was true. She revealed future events with amazing accuracy; but the most fascinating part of her demonstration was when she threw the pen and paper on the floor and the pen began to write without anyone touching it.

These messages told of past events in my life and in the lives of the others who were present. One message said that a man from Pennsylvania would get a diplomatic post the next day, which actually happened. One could speculate and say that the subconscious force of those present grasped the pen or that some disembodied spirit in the next dimension operated the pen. We must remember, however, that people in the flesh, here on this plane, as well as those in the next dimension have a mind and also a body far more rarefied and attenuated than our three-dimensional bodies.

Psychic phenomena are caused by subjective powers and can operate independent of the physical instrument. People in the next dimension do have a subjective mind and they are also in the flesh. ('Flesh' in the Bible means 'embodiment.') This does not refer to tissue, muscle, bone and blood, as such; but we do have bodies to infinity. You can never be without a body.

In the séance room, under scientific investigation, objects have been handled, held and moved completely independent of physical touch. Tables and furniture have been moved around and in one instance in London, I witnessed the washing of dishes without any hands touching them. This is called, in ESP circles, telekinetic energy, i.e., the ability to move objects without the usual physical contact and effort.

Who opened the wine bottle?

Some years ago, while paying a visit to Dr Evelyn Fleet in London, she introduced me to a psychic who was present at the time. Dr

Fleet said that the psychic could serve wine without touching a glass or a bottle. Right in front of our eyes, without anyone touching anything, the wine bottle was opened and a glass was filled to the brim. The glass was held to my mouth, whereupon I confirmed that it was, indeed, *real* wine in a *real* glass.

As Dr Fleet explained, it was the subjective mind of the psychic that had performed this phenomenon. Apparently, she had done this many times before in the presence of Dr Fleet.

There are marvellous powers within us, many of which we have not even dreamed of. One might say that psychic phenomena are caused by fourth-dimensional beings or by the subconscious mind. The point is that all the phenomena are caused by mind power, whether on this plane or the next.

Your subconscious mind can see, hear, feel, smell, travel, touch and taste without the physical organism. You can project yourself thousands of miles, see what is going on and also permit yourself to be seen. Fourth-dimensional or astral travelling is well-known and acknowledged today. To deny that such phenomena exist and that they are experienced by thousands all over the world is downright ignorance.

Why Many Predictions Are Accurate

When you deposit an acorn in the soil, the complete pattern of the oak is already in the acorn. The idea of the full-grown oak must exist in the seed; otherwise, it would never be objectified. The seed undergoes dissolution in the soil. The subjective wisdom proceeds to build up the sturdy oak tree.

When a psychic tunes in on your mind, your thoughts are like seeds. Your mind being timeless and space less, your thoughts and their manifestations are one in mind. In other words, your mind looks upon the thought as completed. Thoughts are things. A good psychic or medium sees the complete manifestation of your ideas before they are objectified on the screen of space.

The medium tunes in on your subjective tendencies, beliefs, plans and purposes and sees them already accomplished. Her subconscious, like your own, reasons deductively only. You could, of course, change her predictions if you so desired by transforming your mind, for changed attitudes change everything.

You Can Be Consciously Aware and Awake

Dr Phineas Parkhurst Quimby, who lived in Maine in the mid-19th Century, was able to condense his identity and appear to people hundreds of miles away. He remained conscious and never entered into a trance in order to read the minds of others or visit them at a distance. He told people the cause of their sickness and how it originated – he also healed many of them. He became clairvoyant by casting out all orthodox and false beliefs and filling his mind with the truths of God.

He performed all his wonderful works in a perfectly normal self-conscious state. Dr Quimby knew that man was independent of his body and that he could function with its counterpart, i.e., his subtle body or astral body, a counterpart for the present one. While conversing with a patient, he could clairvoyantly see another patient a hundred miles away get up from bed and come downstairs completely healed–all this without closing his eyes.

You have another body, which acts independently of the present one. Your mind can operate and move matter. The point is that psychic phenomena occur. Whether it is due to your subconscious mind or to the subconscious mind of a loved one in the next dimension, the thing to remember is that there is but one mind common to all individual men.

POINTS TO REMEMBER

1. Your subconscious is the builder and maker of your body. It controls all the vital functions of your body. It is the seat

of memory and habit. It reasons deductively only. Feed your subconscious with premises that are true and it will respond accordingly. Your subconscious sees without eyes and hears without ears. Within your subconscious are Boundless Wisdom and Infinite Intelligence. In other words, within your subjective depths are all the qualities and powers of God.

2. Your conscious mind is the reasoning, analytical mind. You choose, select, weigh, investigate and reason inductively, deductively and by analogy. Your conscious mind controls your subconscious. Whatever your conscious mind believes and accepts as true, your subconscious will bring to pass.
3. The late Geraldine Cummins, an old friend of mine, practiced automatic writing by getting into a passive, psychic, receptive state, when suddenly her control called 'Astor' would take over. Her hand would be controlled and she would write in foreign languages that she did not understand. She would also bring forth accurate information as well as prophetic utterances that subsequently came to pass. She would move into a semi-trance state and had no idea of what she was writing. In many instances, I do believe that men and women in the next dimension were dictating to her. Moreover, she never had knowledge of the languages in which she wrote.
4. There are many psychics who can tap your subconscious mind while in a perfectly normal, self-conscious state.
5. A certain medium, in a trance state, was able to lift a table and also levitate herself from the ground to the ceiling of the room. I have seen this done several times. An Irish medium, in a trance state, said to a professor who was present that his mother was going to speak to him through her. The mother spoke to her son in Greek and conversed freely with him for about fifteen minutes. He said that he was convinced that it was his mother. In this instance, many materialised forms appeared, many of whom spoke and remained five or six minutes before fading away.

6. Psychometrists can take a ring, a letter or a piece of clothing belonging to a person and accurately describe the person, his characteristics, tendencies, illnesses and also his whereabouts. The reason for this is that the personality of the person is impressed on the ring or article of clothing. The psychic can enter into his innermost thoughts.
7. Many people hear an inner voice warning them of danger and telling them how to protect themselves. Sometimes these warnings come in dreams and visions of the night. A ship's officer made it a habit to instruct his deeper mind that the inner voice would always be to protect, heal and bless him in all ways. In this way, he ruled out false impressions; consequently, it has always been the voice of his Higher-Self.
8. In some seances, when the medium has been in a trance, voices of discarnate entities have seemingly filled the air. I as well as others present, have conversed at length with some of these voices as also have received extraordinarily intelligent answers. I believe that some of the voices have been from the subconscious of the medium, while other voices have come from the next dimension of life. If you hypnotise a man – while in the trance state, suggest to him that he is your brother, he cannot, not knowing your brother, impersonate him in voice, accent, etc.
9. It is quite possible to perceive an apparition of one's loved one immediately prior to transition into the next dimension or soon afterwards. This is based on the intense desire of the loved one to communicate with you. What you see is a projection of the fourth-dimensional body and personality of your loved one.
10. An apparition in the form of a voice or footsteps may well be a thought-form, which means that a person who has met with foul play in the home prior to his death has an intense desire to communicate the manner of his death to someone. The thought-form takes the shape of the personality of the

so-called 'dead person.' When you listen for the message and challenge the thought-form, it disappears – its mission having been accomplished.

11. Black magic, sorcery and malicious malpractice all fall into the same category: negative, destructive thinking and misuse of the law of mind. This negative thinking is based on gross ignorance. Suggestion is a power but not *the* power. *The* Power is the Supreme Intelligence or Living Spirit within you, which is one and indivisible. It moves as harmony, beauty and love. You can reject all negative suggestions and thoughts of others. The suggestions of others have no power unless you give them power. If someone says to you, 'You are going to fail,' you know you are born to succeed, to win. The Infinite within can't fail; therefore, the negative suggestion of the other person simply reinforces your confidence in success and victory. A girl was informed that others were wishing evil on her. She claimed her oneness with the Infinite. She knew God's Love surrounded her to saturate her mind and heart. She gave no power to others but turned her attention to the One Power, which moves as love. The other girls, who were wishing injury and evil for her, were killed in a crash. In other words, they killed themselves. Be sure you wish only what is lovely and of good report for others. What you think and wish for another, you create in your mind, body and experiences.
12. Most automatic writers go into a semi-trance and bring forth marvellous messages of a recondite nature and reveal answers to the most perplexing problems. The automatist holds a pen in her hand. Suddenly her subconscious takes control and proceeds to write without her conscious knowledge. Another fascinating point is that you can see a pen or pencil writing on a piece of paper or slate without being touched by any hand. I have seen this done many times. The automatist claims that messages come from discarnate entities, loved

ones or friends of those present and now living in the next dimension. In many instances, I believe that this is true. You must remember that you will never be without a body. When you read of disembodied spirits or discarnate entities, just realise that what is meant is that they are not functioning in a three-dimensional body but in a fourth-dimensional body. You will have bodies to infinity. There is no reason why you cannot hear from a loved one in the next dimension. They often communicate to loved ones in dreams.

13. It is possible for a very good psychic or medium to open bottles and serve wine in glasses without ever touching the glasses or the bottle. This is one of the powers of your subconscious mind. Actually, your body has no power. It has no self-conscious intelligence, no volition and no initiative–it is characterised by inertia. The power is in your Spirit and Mind.
14. When a sensitive or good psychic tunes in on you, she reads your mind. Your thoughts and their manifestations are one in mind, like the oak is already in the acorn. Your mind is timeless and space less. Your subconscious reasons deductively only. Your thoughts are things. Unless you change your mind, a psychic's predictions should, in most instances, be very accurate, depending on her mental acumen, sagacity and insight.
15. In 1847, Dr Phineas Parkhurst Quimby could condense his identity and appear to patients hundreds of miles away and minister to them. He was able to project his subtle or fourth-dimensional body, which is a counterpart of your present body. He could read the minds of people, tell them the cause of their disease and heal them. He was also clairvoyant. He never went into a trance; rather, he remained conscious. With his eyes wide open talking to patients, he could describe how another patient many miles away was walking downstairs to the dinner table completely healed of an illness or malady.

A FINAL WORD

Tune in on the Infinite Presence and Power within you and claim, feel and know that you are inspired from On High; that the Spirit of the Almighty moves on the waters of your mind and that God thinks, speaks, acts and writes through you. Claim that your words are like apples of gold in pictures of silver and that they are sweetness to the soul and health to the bones. Realise that God loves you and cares for you! Know that His River of Peace fills your mind and heart. Feel that you are immersed in the Holy Omnipresence, flooded with the radiance of the Light Limitless. Believe you now touch the One Who Forever Is and experience that moment, which lasts forever.